ORIENT AND OCEAN

The Chinese Community in Seychelles

Wang Dongxia and Dennis Hardy

First published 2022

© Wang Dongxia and Dennis Hardy 2022

All rights reserved. No part of this publication may be reproduced, stored in a retrieval system, or transmitted, in any form or by any means, electronic, mechanical, photocopying, recording or otherwise, without the prior permission of the publisher.

This book is sold subject to the condition that it shall not, by way of trade or otherwise, be lent, resold, hired out, or otherwise circulated without the publisher's prior consent, in any form of binding or cover other than that in which it is published and without a similar condition including this condition being imposed on the subsequent purchaser.

Enquiries concerning these terms should be addressed to

Blue Gecko Books

bluegeckobooks@ymail.com
www.bluegeckobooks.com

ISBN: 978-0-9575685-5-6

Design and formatting by DevPlus
www.seydevplus.com

Cover photographs
(Front) Collage by Wang Dongxia
(Back) Photo by Jane Woolfenden

Project and Publication

This publication is the outcome of a joint project at the University of Seychelles by members of the Confucius Institute, the Indian Ocean Rim Research Centre for Island Countries based at Dalian University, and the *James R. Mancham* Peace and Diplomacy Research Institute.

Tradition lives on in every society, and many areas of past Chinese experience have an ongoing existence in the present, not only in China itself but in overseas Chinese communities.

Lynn Pan, 'Cultural Origins'. *The Encyclopedia of the Chinese Overseas*. Harvard University Press.

Contents

Acknowledgements — 9
Foreword — 11

Prologue — 13

China Overseas — 15
- The empire within
- Leaving one's homeland
- Textures of Chinatown

Crossing the Indian Ocean — 27
- The remarkable voyages of Zheng He
- The road across the sea
- Ships that pass in the night

Arriving in Seychelles — 37
- Sweet inducements
- Island hopping

People of the Pagoda — 47
- Finding one's way to Benezet Street
- Let the people speak
- Disembarking on the wrong island

Making Good in Paradise — 65
- Tales of good fortune

Community Perspectives — 99
- 'Guides, go-betweens and participants'
- Home and homeland

Epilogue — 109

A Personal Reflection by Wang Dongxia — 115
Notes and References — 117

Acknowledgements

This project would not have been possible without the cooperation and enthusiastic support of many individuals of Chinese and other ancestry in Seychelles, as well as scholars overseas. Our sincere thanks are due to everyone who participated, whether through interviews or sharing documents and ideas.

We would like, firstly, to thank the Vice-Chancellor of the University of Seychelles, Ms Joëlle Perreau, a long-time friend of the Confucius Institute, for her positive interest in this project. She also very kindly agreed to write the Foreword.

In helping us contact various members of the community, and in its recognition of the project, the role of the Chinese Association of Seychelles is much appreciated.

To assist us in many ways, we could not have managed without the willing and enthusiastic involvement of lecturers and volunteers from the Confucius Institute. Special mention is made of Yang Junguang and Luo Na, and also the valued support of Mr Qiao Dejian.

Research of this kind benefits from the earlier work of others. We would especially like to mention the name of Nikita Krivtsov, who kindly shared the results of his own research on the subject. And it was Nikita who brought our attention to research undertaken by Gilles Gerard at the University of Réunion in the early 1990s.

Likewise, we have included in our references the name of Julien Durup, a legendary researcher in Seychelles. We wish we could have followed his example by making our own explorations of the national archives but, unfortunately, these were closed to the public at the time of our research. When these reopen, we hope that future researchers will be able to fill any gaps we have, inadvertently, left.

We warmly acknowledge, too, all those who kindly allowed us to use their various photos, which are separately credited in the respective captions. An appeal, through Facebook, to identify who was present in various group photos from the early days of the community, evoked some informative answers. This generous and invaluable sharing of information is greatly appreciated.

Finally, the project would not have been possible without the support of colleagues at the University of Seychelles. In addition to the Vice-Chancellor, thanks are due to Ms Diana Benoit, Director of the *James R. Mancham* Peace and Diplomacy Research Institute. We would also like to acknowledge the encouragement and interest of Mrs Penda Choppy, Director of the Creole Language and Culture Research Institute.

Our initial intention was simply to report the outcome of the project as a web entry but we were easily persuaded to present our findings in the form of a small book. To do this required its own funding and for this we are deeply grateful to a number of generous sponsors, notably, Mr Jean Weeling-Lee, the Seychelles-China Culture and Tourism Association, the Chinese Association of Seychelles, the University of Seychelles, and, not least of all, the Confucius Institute at the University of Seychelles.

Foreword

Seychelles is blessed with many enviable features. Perhaps one thinks first of the country's unique environment, its beautiful islands fringed with white, sandy beaches and a turquoise sea; not to mention the verdant forests that clothe the slopes of granitic mountains. However, it is not just about place. No less of a treasure is the harmonious mix of people who arrived originally from different parts of the world – from Africa and India, from Europe and the Orient. Together, they form a Creole population, today living in peace, one with another. In a world where it sometimes seems that conflict between races is endemic, Seychelles offers a much-admired exception.

Amongst this mosaic of cultures is a small but influential Chinese community. The first settlers from China came by way of Mauritius. They were followed by others direct from their ancestral homeland, never a large number and, together, not at any time exceeding one percent of the total population of our small island state. One reason why numbers remain small is that it has been common practice to marry across cultural boundaries. This might have resulted in a loss of Chinese identity but that has not happened. Within the community, people invariably think of themselves as Seychellois first yet, at the same time, they never forget their sometimes-distant ancestry. The recent opening of the new pagoda, the Chinese Cultural Centre in the centre of Victoria, is ample evidence of this.

I have always wanted to learn more about this fascinating community. What brought them in the first place to the shores of Seychelles? How have they integrated so well in what must have seemed so different from what they had known before? And why is it that, small in number, they have had such a positive impact on all of our lives? Not only in terms of individuals who have held important positions but also those many Chinese families who set such a good example of citizenship.

The lead researchers in this project were Wang Dongxia, Chinese Director of the Confucius Institute, and Emeritus Professor Dennis

Hardy of the *James R. Mancham* Peace and Diplomacy Research Institute. Both of these institutes are part of the university and I was pleased to learn of their plan to publish this present book, for which I now write the Foreword. An added reason why I am keen to do so is that I have been closely associated with the Confucius Institute from the outset, and I have visited China in the company of both of the authors. *Orient and Ocean* is an appropriate title for a book that tells of a mixing of cultures and I wish it every success.

Joëlle Perreau
Vice-Chancellor
University of Seychelles

Prologue

The provenance of most of the inhabitants of Seychelles can be traced back to Madagascar and the African mainland, from where – in the last quarter of the eighteenth century – they were forcibly brought to work on the new plantations. When slavery was finally ended in the following century, most remained as wage labourers and only gradually were able to diversify their occupations and improve their conditions. Another incoming group, not by then recruited as slaves but with the barely improved status of indentured workers, came from the Indian sub-continent. Control during this early period rested with European colonists, first from France (which in 1770 appropriated the previously uninhabited archipelago in the western Indian Ocean) and then the British. It was not until the latter half of the nineteenth century that a smaller group of immigrants, arriving directly or indirectly from mainland China, were to make their own way as independent settlers to what was still a colony. Over the years, these Chinese pioneers were joined by later waves of compatriots, sharing the same desire to make better lives for themselves and their families.

These five groups – African, Indian, French, British and Chinese – make up most of the present-day population. Its diversity is a dominant feature of the small island state and accounts for a unique Creole character. Respect for this multi-faceted culture is enshrined in the nation's constitution and is a feature of everyday life. In a world ridden with racial conflict, the harmonious mix of different ethnicities in Seychelles is rightly admired.

To find out more about how it works – when so often a combination of diversity and peace is beyond reach – this project tells the story of the Chinese community. The fact that it is the smallest ethnic group in the country is immaterial, as the aim is to see how it has evolved over the years, fitting peaceably into – and contributing to – the wider society.

As such, apart from narrating the unique aspects of the community's history, this is a case study of ethnic cooperation.

There is an added reason why the *James R. Mancham* Peace and Diplomacy Research Institute has combined with the Confucius Institute to undertake this research. Peace is not simply the absence of war – it is rooted in cooperation and an absence of enmity amongst people who go about their everyday business. Our assumption at the start of this project is that the Chinese community is well integrated and relations between those of Chinese ancestry and others in Seychelles are essentially good. It is an assumption that is subsequently borne out by our findings. In a generally troubled world, the story we tell is one that demonstrates how people of different ethnicities really can live peacefully together. It also shows how important community relations are to the architecture of world peace.

China Overseas

As many as sixty million people of Chinese ancestry live outside their original homeland, a number that is more than the total population of many medium-sized nations.[1] Although it is a small proportion of the 1.4 billion who presently live in China, it still represents a remarkable spread of a unique culture. The distribution, however, is far from even; relatively few, for instance, made their way to the western Indian Ocean and, in particular, to the location for this project, the small island state of Seychelles. Compared with other regions, numbers of Chinese are limited but the communities formed still carry with them the distinctive marks of a more extensive diaspora. Time and intermarriage with other ethnicities have diluted the mix, yet (as we will see) a sense of identity with Chinese ancestry remains strong. For that reason, it is important to look, first, at some of the generic characteristics of China overseas.

The empire within

In China, public discussion of empire ('diguo') remains rare. Empire is treated as a pejorative term best directed at others; the word is almost never applied to China itself.[2]

In spite of the extent of the diaspora, much of China's history has been inward looking. The nation has vigorously defended its borders, neither allowing its territory to be eroded nor its cultural traditions weakened. For long periods it has not been expansionist, eschewing the European model of colonization in which foreign lands were forcibly acquired by distant powers. The kind of overseas control exercised elsewhere has not been emulated by Chinese rulers. At the same time, it would be wrong to totally dismiss any association with the term and practices of 'empire'. Ancient China was always referred to in this way, with the ruler taking the title of emperor. But there the similarity with the western notion of empire ends:

> *The Chinese empire was a land-bound empire, controlling vast tracts of land, but China did not expand across the oceans, unlike the French, Spanish, British, Dutch and Portuguese empires. Although Chinese communities have settled in various nations over the centuries, including South Africa, Indonesia, the Philippines and the US, no overseas Chinese empire or colony was created from these Chinese communities.*[3]

For most of its long history, Ancient China remained an 'empire within', inward-looking and governed through the strongly centralized rule of successive dynasties. Its people are predominantly Han Chinese although, within its own borders, this seeming unity embraces a variety of ethnic groups, each of which once boasted its own cultural traditions, dialects and (in a minority of cases) different languages. The roots of this diversity lie in the intricate roots of myriad villages, often with little contact between each other, and the successive layering of different cultures resulting from earlier migrations and invasions by neighbouring powers. Maintaining such a diverse population under unified rule has been a constant challenge for its rulers and is still an issue on the Chinese domestic agenda.

It was not until the latter part of the nineteenth century that the long-held authority of dynasties was seriously questioned. But, for all the changes that were to come, it was not to be the end of an underlying belief that China should continue to be defined by its Han-based identity. Thus, when the modern nation was formed in 1949 – the People's Republic of China (referred to in this text as PRC, or simply China) – this remained a dominant feature. The political system changed but much was still recognizable.

In turn, China has since increased its influence in the outside world. Africa, especially with the ending of colonization and the emergence of newly-independent countries, was ready to adopt plans for development and growth. Not since the legendary navigator, Zheng He, made his voyages across the Indian Ocean at the start of the fifteenth century, has this intriguing continent, for so long beyond the known world, featured so prominently in China's thinking. An important sign of revived interest came in 1996, when the then President of the People's Republic of China, Jiang Zemin, proposed the creation of the Forum on China-Africa Cooperation. Four years later, at the start of the new millennium, leaders of 44 African countries (Seychelles amongst them) were invited to Beijing, where plans were announced for a massive increase in aid and infrastructure projects including new hospitals and schools, as well as training for professionals. An especially welcome feature for the participating member states was the cancellation of outstanding debts and the release of funds to facilitate new loans.[4]

The first ministerial gathering of the China-Africa Forum was held in Beijing in 2000, followed by regular meetings since then
Photo credit: GovernmentZA via Flickr (CC BY-ND)

For newly independent nations, short of investment funds and struggling even to feed their rapidly-growing populations, the offers from China could not have been more timely. China has a policy of supporting African countries by providing interest-free loans and carrying out long-term business investment with no strings attached. Non-interference in internal affairs and mutual support and benefit are principles governing relations with other countries in general, and those in Africa are no exception. Even for those countries which are over-committed and might face short-term debt risks or difficulties with project implementation, China maintains a supportive role. Agreements are designed to overcome such obstacles and achieve success for all parties.

The Chinese approach is markedly different from the old style of European colonization and ongoing American power politics. Instead, China seeks initiatives based on mutual trust, inclusiveness, and the opportunity for all parties to benefit from development. China's growing influence in Africa and the Indian Ocean is underwritten by a desire for peaceful and productive relations.

Leaving one's homeland

The history of the Chinese diaspora is a web of peoples, places, and processes. In particular, the creation of a distinct sense of 'Overseas Chinese-ness' is the product of preservation and adaptation, uniquely bringing together the old and new.[5]

At various times in its history, leaving the country to find a home elsewhere was actually forbidden. At other times, when restrictions were lifted, relatively small numbers of individuals and, sometimes, their families too, have chosen to leave their homeland and go overseas in search of new opportunities. From the 1970s, with reforms and the opening-up of the nation, growing numbers of people have chosen to go abroad to study, to do business, and even to emigrate. Such decisions are made freely by individuals and families rather than by government edict.

In the past, the original migrants left their villages, overwhelmingly, to escape poverty. In good times they could just about eke out a living for their families. But working in the fields was a tenuous existence. Fertile land was scarce in relation to the large number of people it had to support, and adequate yields were dependent on favourable weather to avoid the seasonal impact of drought or devastating floods. Nor was it just a constant battle against the elements, as there were few parts of China that escaped the threat of periodic local wars. Often out of desperation, individual decisions were taken to leave the homeland. Young men would choose in some cases to travel long distances to the nearest port, then paying for rudimentary accommodation on board a junk, or working their passage on a larger vessel *en route* to a faraway place they had only vaguely heard about. Where possible, they took their families with them but it was more likely they were forced to leave their homes as single men.

In the early stages of migration from mainland China, those countries closest to home, bordering the South China Sea and the north-eastern reaches of the Indian Ocean, attracted the greatest number of newcomers. In what is now Indonesia and Singapore, Thailand and Malaysia, Myanmar, Vietnam, and the Philippines, migrant communities were soon established, their numbers peaking at those times when the various economies in that part of the world prospered. Across South-East Asia, Chinese immigrants gradually formed large minorities and, in some cases, they even grew to represent a majority of the local population. In Singapore, for instance, more than three-quarters of the nation's population is of Chinese ancestry. Another example can be found in Penang, on the west coast of the Malaysian

The Chinese community in Penang is the dominant culture
Photo by Jane Woolfenden

peninsula, where the Chinese are the largest ethnic group in the state. Penang is also a good illustration of how groups of migrants would often come from a particular part of China, in this case most being Hokkien people from Fujian and Guangdong, Jiangxi and Guangxi provinces, in the south of their former homeland.

During the nineteenth century, migrants were also lured further afield. Many crossed the Pacific to the distant shores of America's west coast to join the frenzied search for gold and the dream of making an instant fortune. Alternatively, they had little difficulty in finding work as labourers, laying the tracks for some of the great railways which spanned that continent. For both gold-diggers and general labourers, the work was arduous; with very few exceptions, there were to be no quick riches. In time, though, with modest savings, the thought, perhaps, of owning their own shop and engaging in trade loomed larger in their minds. Yet, even with sufficient funds, the way ahead for aspiring immigrants was not easy and often they suffered discrimination from European minorities who were already established in the various townships and resented the arrival of hard-working newcomers. Later, however, successive generations fared well in North America, benefiting from education opportunities and excelling in the professions as well as business; Chinese Americans were to make a major contribution to Canada as well as the United States.

With the formation of the socialist state in 1949, the People's Republic of China, there was at first little in the way of emigration. Following the death in 1976 of Chairman Mao, new opportunities arose and many chose to follow the path of earlier migrants to what were by then developed countries like the United States and Canada (often joining the established communities of their nineteenth-century predecessors), with Australia and New Zealand also becoming popular destinations. In the early years of the present century, relations with Australia were especially strong and a large number of Chinese students entered prestigious universities, with the option of remaining in that country after they graduated.

And, with China's emergence as an industrial nation, many were attracted, too, to countries at a lower level of development, in Africa, South America and western Asia, where newcomers could play a part in economic growth. Skilled by now in the intricacies of international business, the latest arrivals gained a reputation for their financial acumen and entrepreneurial initiatives. In the case of Africa, a feature of the migration process has been the growth of voluntary settlement there, numbering an estimated one million Chinese nationals. Those who took up the challenge were attracted by the prospect of cheap land, trading opportunities and starting new businesses in a continent with a fast-growing, young population.[6]

Elsewhere, new opportunities have been created, attracting a growing number of Chinese immigrants within the region. A good example in the Indian Ocean is the new port of Gwadar on the north-west coast of Pakistan, which marks the western extremity of a major development corridor that will stretch all the way to Karachi in the east, and which has been heralded as a modern gateway into western Asia. To seal the deal, China has proposed the addition of a new hub for international banking and finance, staffed largely by Chinese professionals already skilled in that kind of work. Another project linked to investment is a plan for the construction of a string of man-made islands off the coast of Malaysia, within one of that country's existing economic development corridors. The islands, intended to be settled largely by Chinese professionals, are known as Forest City (also referred to in promotional literature as Country Garden Forest City).[7]

Textures of Chinatown

I'm astounded by people who want to 'know' the universe when it's hard enough to find your way around Chinatown.[8]

One feature of global migration is that new arrivals in a foreign land will tend to cluster in those neighbourhoods where there are already fellow countrymen and women. It is natural enough to do this as that is where they will feel most at home. In such communities they can easily converse in their own language, buy from stores which sell familiar products, get help in finding accommodation and employment, and even, in time, receive loans to start their own businesses.

Chinese migrants were no exception to this general trend and their distinctive communities would typically take on a life of their own. The diaspora has its roots in journeys made from different parts of China, and at first the migrants spoke the unique languages and dialects used in their homeland. When they arrived, they had only the clothes they wore at home, typically loose-fitting tunics made of hemp, with sandals or black fabric 'slip-ons', and often, too, the kind of conical straw hat they might have worn in the fields. Over small fires outside their new homes they boiled rice and mixed it in woks with an assortment of fried vegetables, fish and chicken if available, the exotic smells of their cooking wafting through the lanes. Then, at the time of annual festivals, paper lanterns adorned the buildings – a medley of red, mixed with splashes of gold – and everyone would come together to celebrate the occasion. At the new year, the traditional dragon dance would wind its way round the narrow lanes and squares to bring luck for the year to come. Such communities became ubiquitously known as Chinatown, a familiar form of neighbourhood around the world.

Growth within these original districts was organic. There was no template but, almost instinctively, new settlers saw such places as incomplete without their own pagoda. Spiritually, the pagoda served an underlying belief in Buddhism (although it sometimes made room for Confucianism and Taoism too), a place where its people could pray and participate in religious ceremonies. At the time of a funeral, this is where families and friends would congregate in an act of shared grief, the main room exuding the pungent scents of incense and the gentle sounds of chanting.

Within the pagoda, too, there was always a place for a statue of Guan Gong, a mythical figure revered not only as the Saint of War but also for his loyalty. He is also held in esteem as the God of Wealth and the patron of the numerous trades and occupations that typified the Chinese workforce.

Guan Gong: not only the Saint of War but also the bringer of good fortune
Photo credit: Ihsan Khairir via Flickr (CC BY-SA)

Physically, the distinctive architecture of the pagoda provided a tangible focus for the community, rising above the tiny buildings and narrow lanes that comprised the surrounding area. Pagodas were not confined to China and could be seen in other Asian communities too, but they all shared a characteristic design in the form of a tiered tower with curved roofs sloping upwards at the edge. Often, too, they were brightly coloured, with red or green roof tiles and heavily varnished woodwork. As well as its ritual functions, for families living close by, with little room to call their own, the pagoda also offered an informal space which people could use in different ways – calling in to smoke a cigarette and chat to neighbours, or to drink tea from an ever-steaming urn. Games of cards were played, and the clicking sound of mahjong tiles could always be heard. Children could find a corner to read a book or play games, women to meet and gossip. In different ways, it became a natural hub for the community.

In time, though, two things happened. One is that, with growing confidence and money in their pockets, the community gradually dispersed, with the better-off finding homes in the suburbs or in new apartments downtown. Sometimes the young men will have found a Chinese wife in their community, but often it would be a woman from the host society; in the latter case, these newcomers assimilated more easily, learning a new language and mixing with non-Chinese neighbours as well as their ethnic counterparts. Their original culture was overtaken in many ways, but rarely forgotten.

This kind of transition is not unusual amongst immigrant communities in general. However, in the case of the Chinese, something else occurred. Instead of disbanding what they had created, 'Chinatown' evolved as a continuing hub of activity. People from neighbouring districts and, later, tourists, were attracted to the ethnic restaurants and the colourful boutiques and craft workshops. Some, too, came to gamble or to visit the clubs and houses of ill-repute. While all of this went on, the Chinese themselves retained many of the original business activities, meeting in crowded cafes and in upstairs offices. For relaxation, outside tables would be the scene of lively games of mahjong, with onlookers loudly voicing their advice on what the players should be doing. Although some of the families were by then living elsewhere, others preferred to stay in the area they had come to know. They may long ago have left China but China had not left them.

So, in one way or another, Chinatown remained a working and living community, but at the same time also a tableau displaying a distinctive culture. Pagodas added exotic architecture to what was already so different from the commonplace. Such neighbourhoods are powerful in imagery, for ethnic Chinese a vibrant link to the past, while for visitors a place of seductive colour and activity. Promoted by different municipalities there is no shortage of descriptions to lure even more visitors:

> ... *a kaleidoscope of sounds, smells and colors. The cadence of Chinese dialects fills the air and splashes of red and gold glow from shop windows to banners strung across the narrow streets. The rich smell of roast duck curls out of hole-in-the-wall eating places, blending with the faint smell of incense burning on modest shrines... It's a shopping district; it's a residential neighborhood and it's a tourist destination.*[9]

The general process of settlement might have been comparable from one place to another but, with their diverse origins and destinations, it is hardly surprising that local differences evolved. Chinatown would be recognizable anywhere, but the community in Manila would not be the same as in San Francisco; the Chinatown of Manchester, in the north of England, evolved in different ways from that of Sydney. Climate, language, political requirements and cultural traditions would all create their own nuances. Chinese culture has proved to be adaptive to its surroundings. The situation is invariably dynamic and one must be careful not to create stereotypes for the diaspora:

> *In a globalized world where cultures are constantly in communication, any attempt to label certain groups of people is short-sighted and irrational. Overseas Chinese have continued to explore and build their identities in this increasingly integrated world.*[10]

The differences are important but it is their commonality which tells most about the resilience of Chinese culture.

ORIENT AND OCEAN

Street cooking
Photo by Jane Woolfenden

A modern visitor attraction
Photo credit: Neil Turner via Flickr
(CC BY-SA)

Crossing the Indian Ocean

There is nothing new about the presence of Chinese immigrants in the Indian Ocean, although Seychelles and other small island states in the region have never been the main destination. The number of migrants to our own shores has not been large and it is unlikely that any arrived before the second half of the nineteenth century (mostly not until the last quarter). If, however, one widens the net to include the African landmass, the story is rather different. In that case, Chinese migrants have periodically been drawn to the expansive continent to the west, so different from anything experienced in their own part of the world. The magnetism of Africa continues to have a hold to this day, now attracting a wave of permanent migrants as well as economic investment.

The remarkable voyages of Zheng He

Long before Christopher Columbus, the celebrated Chinese navigator Zheng He travelled through the south and westward maritime routes in the Indian Ocean and established relations with more than thirty countries in Asia, Africa, and the Middle East.[11]

Early in the fifteenth century, when most of the world was still largely unexplored, the legendary Chinese seafarer, Zheng He, led his emperor's fleet into different parts of the Indian Ocean. Setting sail from the South China Sea, he made no fewer than seven expeditions. Although in the previous century a Chinese flotilla under Wang Dayuan had twice ventured into the same ocean and, on the second trip, even reached the East African coast, little in the way of navigation charts and guidance were passed on to possible successors. Thus, for Zheng He, in spite of that earlier experience, his own expeditions were largely journeys into the unknown.

Of Zheng He's seven expeditions, several took him southwards from the Arab countries of what we now know as the Middle East and then along the east coast of Africa, where there is mention of Mogadishu, and possibly on at least one voyage going well beyond this to modern-day Mozambique. Where possible, in these marathon journeys he followed a course within reach of the various coastlines, but on returning to his homeland he ventured north-eastwards across the huge expanse of unmapped waters. In all respects his voyages represented a remarkable feat of navigation and seamanship, not to mention immense courage.[12]

Photo courtesy of Jane Woolfenden

The exploits of Zheng He are renowned, and for the inhabitants of the lands he visited the sight of his fleet approaching would have been awesome. As Admiral of the Fleet, his own ship was a mighty 400 feet in length, and this was matched by other large vessels and an entourage of at least sixty smaller craft in support. For his first expedition the fleet numbered as many as 300, with crews totalling close to 30,000.

But the purpose was at all times largely exploratory, admittedly a show of strength but also a quest for commercial opportunity and political influence for the future. For the lands visited, it was unlikely that most of the inhabitants had previously heard of China; now they would talk of it with wonderment.

Illustration of Zheng He's flagship
Illustration by Kosov Vladimir via Wikimedia Commons (CC BY-SA)

The Yongle Emperor – third ruler of the Ming Dynasty – who sponsored the expeditions, was ambitious in the extreme but even he was alarmed by the mounting expense of it all and priorities closer to home. After the seventh voyage, and Zheng He's death (he died on the return to his home port), Yongle's imperial successor called an end to the venture. In spite of being far ahead of their time, the remarkable exploits of Zheng He were not pursued with the same ambition by others in the following years, and the oriental nation, having shown itself to the world, largely withdrew once again behind its own borders. For many years, China remained something of a mystery to outsiders. Unlike Yongle, successive emperors were not seduced by further expansionist ventures. Their energies were consumed, instead, by the constant challenge of governing a large country that experienced periodic famines and floods; the eternal task of protecting its own borders from outsiders; and, internally, thwarting the machinations of competing warlords. Centuries passed and, though memories must have lingered, this waning of interest in Africa and other parts of the world was left to rest.

Meanwhile, the traffic of ships from other nations continued in the great ocean. Arab traders had been sailing their dhows southwards to East African ports, even before the arrival of Zheng He, and lines of trade were well established. Of greater moment, it was not long after the departure of the Chinese expeditions of Zheng He before the first European explorers, with trade and conquest in mind, appeared round the southern tip of the African continent. Portuguese ships heralded the start of a long and widespread process of colonial conquest, marking a new era in the history of the region. China, at the time, took no part in that – it was not to follow the European example. There were more than enough challenges to engage it within its own boundaries. We have to wait for nearly half a millennium, when the Indian Ocean loomed large again in its thinking, to see a reawakening of interest.

The road across the sea

The development of the Belt and Road is rooted in history, but orients to the future.[13]

From the start of the present century, looking outwards has, indeed, become an integral part of China's rapid development. A lively exchange with other parts of the world has occurred in the course of creating new networks for trade, technology exchange and development. Business representatives make their way to China to explore enticing opportunities and this is reciprocated by comparable visits of Chinese scientists and entrepreneurs to other continents. It has been a remarkable period of growth, a result of which is that China has taken its place as a major power in the modern world.

To encourage and guide what is presented as a mutually beneficial relationship, the present Chinese leader, Xi Jinping, personally put his name to a visionary project for a new network of global infrastructure, generally known as the Belt and Road Initiative. Although the terminology is opaque the concept itself is elegant, giving form to China's aim of concentrating economic relations along strategic pathways. Use is made of the ancient Silk Road to evoke the imagery of transporting ideas as well as goods. Xi Jinping recalls that his home province of Shaanxi, in the west of China, was at the start of the Silk Road, a trail that wended its way across the barren lands of Central Asia, '...and today I can almost hear the camel bells echoing in the mountains and see the wisps of smoke rising from the desert'.[14] In this way, history has been called upon to shape the future.

Images of the ancient Silk Road are evoked to encourage interest in the new concept of Belt and Road
Illustration by Jane Woolfenden

To give more substance to this romantic notion, Xi Jinping used the early opportunity of presidential visits to Kazakhstan and Indonesia to make important pronouncements. In the first, he proposed the revival of the ancient Silk Road through Central Asia and in the second, looking towards the Indian Ocean, he spoke of a new route across the sea.[15] What both pathways had in common was the promise of a series of connected economic nodes that would take development and prosperity to a new level. China would invest in modern infrastructure and trading facilities but it was contended that all parties would benefit. It was a proposal that was hard to resist, setting new goals for global development in the twenty-first century.

No matter how the various corridors of development are defined, it is not disputed that the link with Africa is now a key feature of China's international strategy. The continent is still relatively under-developed; it is rich in oil, minerals and other resources; and a fast-growing population offers the prospect of future markets. Until the second half of the twentieth century, western colonial powers still controlled most of Africa but, one by one, the erstwhile colonies gained independence and emerged as autonomous nations. The map has changed and in many ways the opportunities for development, stimulated by external investment, have increased. While being careful not to repeat the errors of the past and to attract the adverse image of colonial predecessors, China has created a new model of development for the region that is designed to benefit all parties.

In pursuit of a longer-term relationship, China has also been active in offering programmes to improve cultural understanding. Learning the Chinese language, being introduced to the culture, and enjoying the opportunity to undergo training in China are all promoted through Confucius classrooms and institutes. These initiatives are generally appreciated in the recipient countries, especially by the young, for whom the new global alignments that are currently taking shape will become the norm. Unlike the voyages of Zheng He, which proved to be ahead of their time, it is intended that the road across the Indian Ocean today will lead to lasting change based on mutual trust and benefits, in all of the countries embraced by the African continent.

Ships that pass in the night

*One ship sails East, And another West,
By the self-same winds that blow...*[16]

The global extension of China's influence in modern times would not be possible without the parallel development of the nation's merchant shipping fleet; the design of highly efficient containers and associated handling facilities; and the modernization not only of its own ports but also those of its destinations. Shipping, the traditional carrier of goods around the world, has assumed even greater importance in recent decades. Indeed, given the massive increase in the global volume of imports and exports, it has a much bigger role than in the past, accounting, worldwide, for some 90% of all trade. Globalization could not have happened without it. In this context, seaborne traffic across the Indian Ocean exemplifies its vital role. A satellite camera would show that, on any one day, ships are queueing at both ends for entry to the Suez Canal, the vital link between Europe and Asia. Sweeping the stratospheric viewfinder southwards, there is heavy traffic, too, in both directions around the southern tip of Africa; this lengthy itinerary provides a link to and from the markets of South and North America, as well as offering an alternative route to Europe. And from the Middle East, in spite of reserves in other parts of the world (and the environmental rhetoric of moving away from fossil fuels), the Gulf continues to generate a constant flow of oil tankers through the Strait of Hormuz and into the Indian Ocean, then to points east and west.

For China, these various shipping lanes are the lifeblood of its fast-growing economy. It is highly dependent on imports of oil and other natural resources (increasingly from Africa), and on the safe passage of shipping to carry its exports. In its ports along the South China Sea, containers piled high and the presence of massive oil and other refineries tell their own story. To guarantee these flows is probably the most important logistical challenge it has to face, and at the heart of its plans must be an understanding of geography. One thing that is immediately obvious is that there are points of vulnerability which need to be protected.

Thus, the natural shipping lane from China westwards takes traffic close to Singapore and then north-west through the narrow Strait of Malacca. In normal times, this is not a concern and, once through the Strait, ships make their way across the open sea. But what if times are not normal? What if, at a time of international tension, this natural route is blocked? In that kind of situation, the whole of its economy would be threatened. The fact is that China has become reliant on the uninterrupted passage of shipping on the open seas. Quite apart from safeguarding its huge investments in the region, its dependence on the free flow of both imports and exports makes this a national priority. In this situation, China is aware of its vulnerabilities. The Strait of Malacca is the most obvious 'chokepoint' but there are other places which could pose a threat too: notably, the Strait of Hormuz, the Suez Canal and the Mozambique Channel. When pirates threatened the security of shipping off the coast of Somalia, China was quick to join other naval powers to contain, if not to remove, these illegal actions. Keeping the seas open is integral to the very process of global trade in general and to China's economic growth in particular. The coronavirus pandemic from 2020 showed all too well what can happen if existing flows are disrupted.

With so much at stake, China needs to support its merchant shipping in the region with naval escort fleets. The sea lanes are China's arteries and the risk of traffic being curtailed simply cannot be contemplated. In response, year on year, China has brought more of its support ships into the ocean. It has done this, knowing that the logistical challenge is immense. When, for instance, strategists decided to deploy more escort fleets in the Indian Ocean, they had to factor in the challenge of distance to and from their home ports. Only through careful planning and dedicated investment would a long-term commitment to this use of maritime support be possible. From the ports of South China to the east coast of Africa, ships have to travel up to 10,000 kilometres; even to and from the Middle East it is at least half that distance. To give adequate support, there must be secure ports in the region with the resources to offer, at a minimum, the means for light repairs and refuelling. In addition to relying on these, a key part of China's strategy has been to establish its own, well-equipped military base in Djibouti, on the Horn of Africa.

Chinese container ships are the main link between local producers and global consumers
Photo by Roel Hemkes via Flickr (CC BY)

Elsewhere in the region, large-scale investment has led to the modernization of traditional ports and the introduction of new infrastructure. As already mentioned, a classic example is the new port of Gwadar, in the extreme south-west of Pakistan, abutting the border with Iran and located as close as possible to the Gulf. It is itself a massive project, geared to merchant shipping in the Indian Ocean, as well as associated development along the coast. But it is by no means confined to the seaboard, being linked inland as part of major infrastructure investment strategy to support China's economic drive through central Asia.[17] In spite of poor operational management by the Sri Lankan authorities, leading to a bail-out by the Chinese investment company and a renegotiation of the terms of the original agreement, the development is now on course to be fully functioning by the end of 2022.

With increased activities, such as the above, along the coast of southern Asia and through the ports of East Africa, the map of the Indian Ocean is being redrawn. Ships ply in all directions, the source of a busy network of trade between nations, with China playing a key role. Outsiders read into this what they may. For some, it means a welcome increase in growth and development from which all can benefit; others, however, see it as an intrusion into what they have for long regarded as their own, exclusive domain. As authors of this book, we have chosen to stand aside from this complex world of geopolitics, with its chilling talk of a new Cold War. Our focus, instead, is on the lives to be found in just one oceanic community, namely the people of Chinese ancestry in Seychelles.

If one can learn anything from history, it is that ordinary people want nothing more than to go about their lives in peace. This is why, in the following chapters, we will talk of Chinese loyalty to their adopted homeland; let nations vilify each other and we will seek the enduring qualities of community and friendship; let others vie for newfound power and we will value the long routes of tradition. Or, to put it another way, our aim is to let the Chinese community speak for itself, to respect the views of its people and the lives they have made for themselves on these distant islands.

Arriving in Seychelles

So how did it all come about? What led small groups of people from a faraway land to find their way to a remote archipelago that was, until the third quarter of the twentieth century, a European colony? Did it prove to be a good move or not? Was there a place for Chinese migrants in Seychelles? Were they able to improve their lives?

Sweet inducements

By the 19th Century, sugar was considered a necessity. This evolution of taste and demand for sugar had major economic and social implications for the entire world. As a result of this demand, tropical islands were colonized and sugar cane plantations began 'cropping up' in record numbers.[18]

The Chinese diaspora is in some ways a map of economic opportunities in different parts of the world. It is a map which shows where migrants have gone to live in the hope of better conditions than they had known before. Mauritius, in the western Indian Ocean, was one such place.

It was Mauritius rather than Seychelles which first attracted Chinese migrants to this distant region. They were lured by the fast-growing sugar cane industry on the island, which prospered in response to the sweet tastes of European markets. Later, a minority of Chinese settlers were encouraged to move again, this time northwards across nearly 1,800 kilometres of open seas to the archipelago of Seychelles. In time, newcomers were to bypass the early staging post of Mauritius and migrated direct to Seychelles.

Of the European nations, first the Dutch and then the French were attracted to the large island of Mauritius that lies just within the tropics. Sugar cane production was started in a relatively small way by the Dutch (mainly with a view to use it as the key ingredient in a distilled alcoholic drink, *arrack*). The French then took control of the island early in the eighteenth century, renaming it Isle de France (*Île de France* in modern French) and, by using slave labour, they developed the first large-scale plantations. In turn, the French were ousted by the British in 1810, who restored the original Dutch name of Mauritius. When slavery was abolished in British colonies in 1835, indentured workers were brought from India to work in the fields and in the nearby factories where the crop was processed. For more than a century, sugar cane was the lifeblood of the economy.

In the early years of French occupation, migrants were forbidden from entering the colony unless they agreed to work in the plantations. When this was replaced by a system which allowed a choice of employment, Chinese migrants found the prospects more attractive. There was less interest in working directly with sugar cane than in providing some of the infrastructure and services that sustained this core activity. Homes needed to be built, links improved to the ports, and (in spite of their low level of income) the basic needs of the workers in the plantations had to be met. As a result, the Chinese opened small shops selling a limited range of goods, the kind of place where an egg or a cigarette could be bought singly, and, even then, sometimes on credit. As well as locating themselves across the island, close to the main plantations, many of the newcomers congregated in the capital, St Louis, where a small version of Chinatown took shape.

The earliest arrivals from China came from the south-east province of Guangdong. Although the control of Mauritius changed hands, that made no apparent difference to the Chinese community, which grew steadily in the first half of the nineteenth century to around 5,000 in number. After that, there were dips in this total when – due to a combination of cyclone damage, plant disease, and price falls in world markets – the sugar cane industry suffered periodic setbacks. There was also discontent amongst the Chinese settlers that they were at first unable to own land. As a result, some were encouraged by their families to move elsewhere within the region, including to Seychelles; the 1880s saw the first organized exodus, when a group of twenty or so left for the colony to the north. But those who remained (equivalent then to roughly 3% of the Mauritian population) prospered in their own businesses, specializing in construction, retail and wholesale trade, and port facilities.

After many years of steady growth, numbers in Mauritius were boosted towards the end of the twentieth century, when China embarked on its pro-Africa policy of economic development, opening the way for a new generation of business-minded immigrants. In Chinese eyes, the western Indian Ocean now assumed a new level of importance. Before this latest phase, however, records of how the Chinese found their original niche occupations remain piecemeal, although one intriguing piece of recent research is based on the memories of elderly residents. This can only take one back to the early twentieth century but even that is enough to offer a glimpse of a previous era. It tells, for instance, that on the Queen Victoria sugar estate:

> *There were 3 Chinese shops in the village. Liw sen, Lee Wong Chung and la boutique Andrey. People purchased on credit and they pay when they get the salary at the end of the month. Everyone had a 'carnet ration' of red colour in which the Chinese shopkeeper kept his records of things which the customer purchased.*[19]

For a more comprehensive picture of what the Chinese community did, and how a small number left Mauritius for Seychelles, we are greatly indebted to the archivist and author, Huguette Li-Tio-Fane Pineo, for her seminal work on the diaspora (of Indians as well as Chinese) in the Indian Ocean.[20] Mauritius, she shows, was the first port of call for most of the Chinese immigrants (following an unsuccessful attempt to relocate indentured Chinese workers who had previously settled in Sumatra). Part way between Asia and Africa, the island offered a kind of base camp, an opportunity to get used to the alien environment and culture of the region, 'a haven where they paused to learn Western ways of living and Western languages before continuing on their journey to a more hostile clime'.[21]

The Chinese community was well thought of in Mauritius and, in the words of the British governor of that colony in 1871, the people 'are thorough citizens of the world and have no prejudices of race; they rapidly assume the manners, dress and, in name at least, the religion of the country they inhabit'.[22] It seems that the Mauritian governor was sceptical about the adoption of Christianity by Chinese migrants, but in time he was proved wrong. Not only were the various congregations thriving, but individual members of Chinese ancestry were to assume important roles in both the Catholic and Anglican churches.

Although the Chinese community in Mauritius had even in the nineteenth century become well established, some individuals were already looking beyond the horizon. By encouraging some of their own kind to start new settlements elsewhere in the region, it was argued that an effective commercial network could be developed across the Indian Ocean, from which all would benefit. It was their business acumen and entrepreneurial spirit that was most valued, an obvious point that one governor of Seychelles missed entirely when he wrote to his counterpart in Mauritius asking if Chinese market gardeners could be sent to his own islands. The request was met with nothing less than a sharp rebuke:

> *Where within five degrees of the line would you see a 'potato' unless it be imported from cooler climes? Even cabbages are apt to turn yellow at the equator... But here where is one to get hold of the Chinese? All the celestials here are shopkeepers not gardeners.*[23]

The Seychelles governor was clearly unaware of how times had moved on as the former generations of migrants, who had previously known only the land, were by then more interested in commerce:

> *By the end of the 19th century, about 81.3% of the Chinese population in Mauritius were likely traders.*[24]

Few would have been attracted at that stage by the prospect of returning to back-breaking work in the fields. They were to find other ways to improve their lives in Seychelles.

Island hopping

... there is a better life, a better world, beyond the horizon.[25]

Beneath the surface of the western Indian Ocean is a complex geological platform which connects Mauritius to the neighbouring islands of Rodrigues and Réunion. Less obviously, a submerged plateau extends northwards some 2,000 kilometres from Madagascar to Seychelles. This interconnected geology (under the name of Mascarene) is matched by its ethnic geography, in which different groups have moved from one island to another. So it was that in 1886 a small number of Chinese left Port Louis in Mauritius to make the choppy sea crossing to Seychelles, alighting after several days at the port of Victoria. Having lived in Mauritius, they were already familiar with the kind of Creole culture they could expect and were ready to start their new lives.

Unlike what they had known before, where the large sugar plantations encouraged dispersal across the country, the newcomers tended to congregate in Victoria, on the main island of Mahé. The first recorded arrival of a Chinese migrant was not until 1863, and more than twenty years passed before a group of twenty-three followed.[26] This was the real start of the Chinese community in Seychelles. The newcomers quickly found niche opportunities in different aspects of buying and selling. With children given the job of collecting parcels, running errands, and then minding the shop when their parents were out, businesses could be open for long hours and operate with low overheads. The American sociologist, Burton Benedict, included Seychelles in his field visits and concluded that family firms are an effective part of a developing economy, closely embedded in the local culture.[27] The adage, 'family firms and firm families' has been used more than once in our interviews with the Chinese community.

Even today, there are shops in Victoria which retain pioneer family names such as Kim Koon, Ahoye and Weeling. Family firms suited the circumstances at the time, when it was common to have many children, yet also when access to capital was limited. In the face of competition from the Indian community, as well as from fellow Chinese, Affoi &

Company emerged as the largest of the general merchants. By the turn of the century, a few entrepreneurs left Mahé to look for further opportunities on the other inner islands, especially La Digue.[28]

The traditional pattern of a business on the ground floor and living space above can still be seen in Weeling Lee's shop in Mont Fleuri
Photo by Qiao Dejian

Nor was the contribution of the new migrants restricted to trade, as some brought with them unique skills from their earlier lives. For instance, an immigrant known as Sheng was the first in Seychelles to distil the plantation crop of cinnamon. Another pioneer was Joseph Kim Koon who, with his family, used coconut oil as a basic ingredient in the local manufacture of soap. Even bakeries were new to the colony, and a debt is owed to Lai Lam for introducing specialist shops selling bread and cakes, a novelty at first but soon to become the norm.

From modest beginnings, year by year the Chinese community in Seychelles grew. By the 1930s the total was around 300. Numbers have never been large, probably at no time more than a thousand, equivalent at most to 1% of the nation's population. Yet, in spite of this small proportion, it has proved to be an influential group. Various individuals have risen to positions of prominence while others, who may not be so well known, have quietly got on with their lives, contributing in different ways to Seychelles society. They have integrated well and are respected for their loyalty, family life and sense of community.

Kim Koon's shop in Victoria, 1981
Photo courtesy of Bernard Perroud

The Chinese identity survived, in spite of the fact that most of the early migrants were single men who often married local women of a different ethnicity. There were good reasons for 'marrying out' and, even as late as the 1930s, Chinese men in the community outnumbered women by five to one.[29] The Seychelles historian, Julian Durup, has compiled a fascinating study of marriages that took place amongst the first cohort of migrants, up to 1905, showing that the overwhelming number of men in the community chose a non-Chinese wife. There was obviously a penchant, too, for a wife who was sometimes considerably younger than the husband.[30]

When free education became available in Seychelles after 1977, the Chinese community took full advantage of the new opportunities. Education continues to this day to be highly valued and young people (until recently, sons more than daughters) have always been encouraged within their families to work hard, resulting in a high rate of entry to the local colleges and then continuing their studies at a university overseas.[31] Anxious parents, who had been all too familiar with poverty and the long hours of running a shop, urged their children to train for the professions. Once qualified, it was not uncommon for their offspring to settle in advanced nations, like the US and Canada, the UK and Australia. Not everyone followed that path and those who returned to Seychelles on completing their education would either enter one of the professions or, instead, they would take on managerial roles or run their own business. Either way, the well-qualified individuals were invariably accomplished in English and often, too, in French and/or another language but, over time, few would be able to understand Mandarin (the most widely spoken variety of Chinese and now regarded as the official language of China).

While there was always a general consensus that education was important, there was also a case for a dedicated Chinese school, where Mandarin would be taught. With each year that passed, there was a perceived danger that more members of the community would lose the ability to communicate in the language of their forebears. Not only language but also religion, with the traditional faiths of Buddhism, Taoism and Confucianism giving way to Christianity (mainly Catholicism). What kind of Chinese ancestry would it be if few people could understand the most commonly-used language in what was still regarded as their homeland? And how would their culture survive if they also lost touch with their traditional religions?

The request for a Chinese school surfaced from time to time, and was argued most strongly towards the end of the Second World War. Led by the Chinese Association, it was explained to the authorities that:

> *... the Association was very worried by the fact that the local Chinese children did not know their own language and often did not recognize themselves as Chinese... A nation has her independence of character as a man possesses his instinctive personality. The ideas of ethics, mode of life and customary law of the Chinese are different from those of foreigners. Therefore, a Chinese type of education is the most urgent need for our community.*[32]

The advocates even identified a teacher in China, who they wanted to bring to Seychelles so that a start could be made. It was argued that space in the pagoda could be used, at least initially, for a schoolroom. No matter how convincing their case, however, it met stiff opposition from colonial officials. The justification for a separate school was countered by the argument that it was surely better to teach in English as the *lingua franca* and to instil British values, rather than to diffuse learning amongst the various minorities. What would happen if they all wanted their own school? Colonial rule was not receptive to this kind of cultural exception, nor in time was the postcolonial socialist regime in Seychelles, but by then in any case the sense of urgency had lessened. Pragmatism became the order of the day, with an acceptance (albeit with some reluctance) of the decision that a special school would not be allowed. At least there remained the freedom to learn a traditional Chinese language if desired, a challenge to which the Confucius Institute has responded. Beyond a basic level, however, very few take the opportunity to do so.

One thing that has not changed, however, is a continuing interest in Chinese cuisine, very much a part of traditional culture but also much loved by people from other ethnic groups. To illustrate this, no account of the Chinese community would be complete without reference to Dang Kow, who (a few years after his father) made his own journey to Seychelles in the 1950s.[33]

He recalls that from Hong Kong he travelled to Bombay and then by a slow boat (no doubt calling in on every port *en route*), on a voyage that lasted fifty-two days. When he finally arrived in the port of Victoria, he took whatever jobs were going, including the tedious task of counting coconuts. He was seen as reliable and it was not long before he was asked to manage a small shop at Mahé's Grand Anse. This was an opportunity not to be missed, and he would get up at 4 am every morning to bake bread and cakes before the shop opened. Nothing was easy and he walked over the mountains of La Misère to buy provisions in Victoria. Even a pair of canvas shoes was barely within his means. His sights, however, were set on one day opening his own restaurant. To learn more about Chinese cooking he revisited Hong Kong and spent three months in various kitchens.

By then, in 1975, he was ready to realize his dream, in the form of a restaurant with the name of King Wah (meaning 'good atmosphere'), in Benezet Street, close to the pagoda. He introduced for the first time, dishes that were later to become mainstream on the menu, like sweet and sour pork, chow mein and his own speciality, King Wah chicken. Customers enthused about his authentic cooking and his takeaway service was renowned for its pork noodles. Sadly, he passed away in 2021, before we were able to hear his story firsthand but it is clear from those who knew him that Mr Dang is recalled with affection and his cooking acknowledged as one of the treasures of the community.

Dang Kow
Photo courtesy of Chinese Association Seychelles

People of the Pagoda

If only to survive in their new environment, migrants in any situation have to recognize and adapt to their new surroundings. Those who expect everything to be the same as the life they had known before will struggle. In contrast, newcomers who are sensitive to the ways of their adopted country, and are willing to learn, will generally fare well. On balance, Chinese migrants have achieved a carefully honed balance between long-held traditions they have brought with them from their original homeland, and the challenges of embracing a new culture.

Finding one's way to Benezet Street

[La pagode...] située rue Benezet, dans le petit quartier commerçant, elle signale au promeneur l'existence d'une minorité au même titre que la mosque et le temple indien dans les rues avoisinantes.[34]

A pagoda makes a statement. For those of Chinese ancestry, it offers a daily reminder of their provenance; for the rest of society, it tells of the presence of a distinctive community. The original pagoda (referred to in the above quote), dating from 1898, was located in Benezet Street and the new one has replaced it on the same site. It is as near to the centre of Victoria as one could find.

One might have thought that this is where the community was originally clustered, and this was certainly the case for some of the early migrants. But not all. The fact is that the newcomers were by no means united. They identified either as Cantonese or Hakka and at first often behaved as rivals rather than fellow countrymen and women: *'un véritable antagonisme entre les deux 'tribus'*.[35] Partly this was because they each spoke a different language, making communication difficult, but they also invoked their separate histories. As a result, while the Cantonese congregated in the centre, close to the small market, the Hakka settled a kilometre or so to the south, in the area of Mont Fleuri. Numbers were few in any case and, because of this separation, there has never been the kind of thriving Chinatown one finds elsewhere in larger settlements.

The original pagoda in Benezet Street
Photo courtesy of Nikita Krivtsov

At first, the Cantonese and Hakka communities each formed their own club in the two areas of Victoria where they had settled. They soon came to realize, however, that the building of a pagoda, which they both wanted, would require their combined resources. It must have taken a monumental effort, so soon after their arrival in Seychelles, but in just a few short years the two-storey building was ready to use. A later description tells of what it could offer:

> *This pagoda is a stone built, solid structure of two-storeys. The large downstairs room is used for a Social Club for Chinese, while the corresponding room upstairs is used as a Church, where Chinese worship is conducted under the tenets and teaching of Confucius. In this*

People of the Pagoda

room is a large central carved erection of a seated image of Kwang Tai, disciple of Confucius and preacher of his doctrines. Before this shrine, and a smaller one, incense sticks are burnt and offerings are placed.

A large central table has an intricately carved front, gilt, and apparently modern, with figures of all kinds, including fishes [sic], crabs and crayfish. In many of the carvings, the sun occupies a central position at the top. There are some halberds with carved metal top pieces.[36]

Most of all, the pagoda offered a sense of community, or at least it did when the migrants were still settling in. The pagoda was originally central to the life of newcomers: in a religious sense, a place where people could come to pray and get married, or, on an everyday basis, somewhere to meet friends informally, to cook Chinese food and to celebrate traditional events during the year. Over time, the essential role of the pagoda in the community has diminished. As an illustration of this, an observer in the early 1990s was sceptical about its continuing

The new pagoda, opened in 2022
Photo by Wang Dongxia

purpose. He noticed that on the walls in the various rooms were pictures of China but none were religious.[37] The rooms themselves, he observed, were not well looked after. People came in and out of the building but they saw it primarily as a place for informal leisure, as little more than a community hall.

In spite of these doubts, when the surviving pagoda was demolished in 2014 the community felt there was something missing in their lives. As a result, after a protracted period of construction, a new pagoda was completed in early 2022. It had been delayed repeatedly by the practical difficulties of fitting the new building into a tightly-constrained site, and the burden of rising costs. The financial challenge was formidable but, in the end, the community banded together with loans and gifts to settle outstanding accounts. The new building stands on the same site as its predecessor, in Benezet Street, opposite the main market, in the very centre of Victoria.

A high-profile opening was postponed because of coronavirus restrictions at the time but that was not to stop discussions within the community about how it could best be used in the future. Loosely based on a traditional design it is now intended, not so much as a place of worship (although there is provision for that too) but, rather, a broad-based cultural centre for use by local Chinese residents and other Seychellois. It offers rooms for meetings and events, with opportunities to learn about and enjoy some of the traditions practiced in their ancestral homeland, as well as a place to find out about modern change in China. Collaboration with the Confucius Institute will enable language classes and a range of other activities. These are still early days, but it is expected that it will become a hub for a more diverse community than was the case with the pagoda in the past.

The driving force behind the new pagoda has been the Chinese Association, a voluntary organization that is, typically, to be found in most communities in the diaspora. Its basic aim in Seychelles has been to uphold cultural values and traditions as an essential feature of ethnic diversity in the country. As well as offering its members a chance to raise issues of common interest, close links are maintained with the

Seychelles government and with the Chinese Embassy in Victoria. In formal terms, the purpose of the association is:

- *to create awareness, to inform, to educate, to support, to promote, and to advocate on issues of interest to the Chinese community and its descendants;*

- *to encourage participation, to provide a forum for involvement, to empower the Chinese Seychellois in the cultural, economic and social processes;*

- *to represent the Chinese Seychellois population in their common causes and to ensure Chinese representation in the social, cultural and economic life of Seychelles;*

- *to share and enjoy the commonality of experiences and to identify and celebrate the differences among Chinese Seychellois; and*

- *to recognize, foster, and nurture outstanding achievements and contributions of Chinese Seychellois.*[38]

Most of the present members are unfamiliar with Mandarin and the business of the association is conducted in Creole or English. In contrast with members whose families have been here for a generation or more, an influx of more recent arrivals in Seychelles are Chinese speakers. Their agenda is different from that of the established community and, to respond to their own priorities, a separate organization, the Trade Promotion Association, was formed in 2014. It has fewer members than the older association but it performs a more sharply-defined role and business is conducted in Mandarin. For its members, there is less interest in cultural traditions and more in modern business opportunities, although it is anticipated that this will change if their children attend local schools and mix beyond their immediate community. It is known, however, that some of the latest migrants intend to move on to other locations in the region or even to return to China.

ORIENT AND OCEAN

The photo overleaf shows members of the Association, shortly after the end of the Second World War, with Sir Selwyn Clarke, Governor of Seychelles at the time. Sir Selwyn was a good friend of the Chinese community, recalling the comfort he received from local people following his release from captivity as a Japanese prisoner of war.

Members of the Chinese Association circa 1950, outside the old pagoda
Photo courtesy of Robert Chong Seng

Let the people speak

I have never been to China and cannot speak Mandarin. I regard myself as Seychellois. But I think it's important to keep the traditions alive.[39]

To find out more about how migrants have adapted, we asked various individuals to share their own histories of living in Seychelles. Do they any longer feel they are Chinese, or are they now Seychellois? Does this balance between different cultures change over time? In this section we record our conversations with longstanding residents who are now acknowledged as part of the local culture, contrasting this with the experience of more recent arrivals.

In the absence of a recognized Chinatown, 'people of the pagoda' is used metaphorically to describe the original clusters of migrants, not only in the centre of Victoria but also in Mont Fleuri. The newcomers arrived by sea, alighting in the nearby port, and it was natural enough to find a place to live where there was already a Chinese community. This had the advantage not only of being able to find a job amongst people with a common background but also the offer of security in a strange land. Although the original concentrations have largely dispersed, the term has a meaning beyond geography, conveying a sense of ordinary life – where people of Chinese ancestry would shop, conduct various businesses, and come together for cultural events.

Through the good offices of the Confucius Institute, contact has been made with a variety of residents who are at the heart of everyday life in the community, and questions were asked about their present way of life and sense of identity. Where possible, the interviews were face-to-face but (mainly because of Covid restrictions at the time) some were undertaken by phone and email. The language used was sometimes English but also Mandarin.

Specifically, twenty-five interviews were conducted over a couple of months in 2021, with a view to talking to a reasonable cross-section of Chinese society in Seychelles.[40] Of the individuals interviewed, the oldest was aged seventy and the youngest seventeen. All of the respondents regarded themselves as being of pure Chinese descent. Fifteen are from families that have been in Seychelles for more than one generation, while ten are new immigrants. Other than these general characteristics, the main findings were as follows:

- Sixteen of the interviewees were themselves, or through their families, originally from Guangdong, a coastal province in the extreme south-east of the country; the rest came from other provinces, including Liao Ning, Hu Bei, Fu Jian and Hu Nan.

- Fourteen were born in China and eleven in Seychelles.

- Significantly, those who were born in this country regard

themselves as Seychellois (albeit with a keen sense of their Chinese ancestry), whereas those who have only recently arrived and who were born in China remain firmly Chinese.

- Those who come from families which have lived in Seychelles for two or more generations have adapted well to the local culture, including through the use of the Creole language and often English as well. They have a shared experience of attending the country's schools and colleges, growing up and mixing with fellow Seychellois of different ethnicities.

- In contrast, those who were born in China have not (at least so far) adapted so well. Language problems make it hard to mix not only with Seychellois but also with second-generation Chinese. They prefer to eat their own cuisine and have little interest in local news; as a generalization, they are primarily focused on business and maximizing their income. Integration within the wider community is not their priority, not least of all because they are not sure how long they will stay.

- Language is an important signifier of identity and assimilation. Those who are second-generation (or more) will normally speak two languages, English and Creole – but none of them are familiar with standard Mandarin. A few can speak a little Hakka or Cantonese (two varieties of Chinese) amongst their families. The Confucius Institute offers classes in Mandarin but only a small minority take advantage of these. The inability to speak the languages of their original homeland may sometimes affect personal links to family members who remain there, and will undoubtedly be a barrier to their understanding of ongoing developments in China. In contrast, newcomers continue to speak Mandarin and are less likely to be familiar with Creole.

- In spite of their inability to follow events in China in their original language, second and earlier generations celebrate traditional festivals and other events which bring them together. The Spring Festival, for example, reminds them of how families and friends in their homeland would wish each other good fortune for the coming year, of how their homes and streets would be colourfully decorated, and how various delicacies would be prepared to mark the occasion. Both the Chinese Association and the Confucius Institute play an important part in keeping this traditional time of celebration alive. In turn, the Chinese Embassy supports the organization of China Day as another way to encourage a sense of common identity.

In addition to the direct answers to questions, four further findings became apparent. One is that, although all of the respondents considered themselves Chinese, there is still a readiness to recall their different cultural backgrounds. Those who regard themselves as Cantonese, for example, point out that their own language could not be understood by Mandarin-speaking Chinese and that this led to a separation between them and other communities. Language differences in the community are no longer an issue as most contemporaries will speak Creole and English, although this history is not forgotten.

Of greater significance is the collective perception of the Hakka, the largest source of early migration to Seychelles. The Hakka are Han Chinese who originated in north-central China and then, over a long period, migrated south to escape the chaos caused by internal wars, and to seek better conditions. For many, their long journey south ended in the coastal province of Guangdong, where they became the majority group.[41] Because they had been repeatedly forced to move, they would invariably find themselves farming some of the poorest land. As such, they gained a reputation for their hard work and strong character, qualities that are often referred to with pride by present-day Hakka. Their propensity to migrate also led to their being named 'guests', borne out not only by internal moves but also by overseas migrations. From the ports in Guangdong, it was relatively easy to join others on ships bound, initially, for countries in South-East Asia. Like other second and later-generation migrants, their original language was soon forgotten although a consciousness of their background remains. Cantonese and Hakka sometimes recall their rivalry in the early days although this barely surfaces now.

A second interesting finding that emerged only indirectly is the sharp difference between those Chinese who have lived in Seychelles for two or more generations and those who arrived more recently. The one has its roots in a traditional past, when China was a rural society with deep-rooted customs; the other is linked to the modernization and rapid development of the global nation. China's links with countries in Africa are especially relevant to this latter wave of migration to Seychelles, with the Indian Ocean emerging as a focus of strategic interest (referred to earlier as a road across the sea). The two groups are different in many ways, including their provenance, with the early settlers coming mainly from the south-east while the former homes of newcomers are more widely dispersed. They are attracted by business opportunities, especially in activities like construction, fish exports and trade. They started to arrive in the 1970s, with the first phase of the opening of the Chinese economy, increasing rapidly towards the end of the 1990s. Unlike their predecessors, they generally have no plans to remain in Seychelles. Often, they will have families in China, make regular visits home, and follow the news in Mandarin. Their interest in the established Chinese community in Seychelles is limited.

It remains to be seen whether the two groups – the old and new – will, in time, find common ground. Much depends on whether the newcomers decide to stay and make Seychelles their home. If they do, they will invariably learn Creole and send their children to schools where they will mix with classmates from other ethnic groups. As such, the present gap will narrow and the Chinese community will evolve along more uniform lines. But, at this stage, few seem to think that will happen.

Thirdly, one cannot ignore the different attitudes and values of young people who have grown up in Seychelles, who (like young people everywhere) will not necessarily follow the same paths as their parents. To the youth in the community, China is part of their parents' history. They may well respect this and join them on festive occasions but it will probably not be their main point of reference; they are likely to learn more from their peers and global networks than from older generations. It is not that they will deny their Chinese ancestry but that it will not necessarily be so important in their fast-moving lives.

Finally, as something of a footnote to a generally positive account of the emergent community, it is only fair to point out that not everyone was necessarily a paragon of virtue. Families in the community who are rightly praised for their determination to make things work will also tell of the lure of gambling, or of men who left behind a wife and children in China to start a new life in Seychelles. Such are the frailties of human nature and it would be doing a disservice to the majority of good Chinese citizens to pretend there were no exceptions.

Disembarking on the wrong island

I once read a silly fairy tale, called 'The Three Princes of Serendip': as their Highnesses travelled, they were always making discoveries, by accident and sagacity, of things which they were not in quest of. [42]

Migrants from China would have had numerous tales to tell of the arduous voyage across the Indian Ocean. One of the most intriguing themes is that some of those travelling from China will have arrived in Seychelles by accident, the outcome of an unexpected turn of events that would take their lives in directions that were never intended. Sometimes the ship they were sailing with developed engine troubles, preventing it from continuing to a more distant destination and forcing a lengthy delay for repairs in Victoria's harbour. There were also instances of contagion on board, which led to the removal of passengers for periods of quarantine on one of the inner islands of Seychelles. Originally bound for Madagascar or the African mainland, some of the indisposed travellers decided to remain in Seychelles and seek their fortune here. It was a case of serendipity, an unexpected and unplanned event that could well turn out to be in their best interests. One such story is that recounted by Paul Chow about the arrival of his father and how he stayed to make his own contribution to his new country.[43] In the original issue of the newspaper where this appeared (of which he was at the time its editor), the memoir is headed 'The life story of a Chinese migrant who made Seychelles his home away from home'. It is a fascinating and well-told story that is unique, but which in different ways will resonate with the recollections of other families who were also to settle permanently in Seychelles.

Paul Chow records that his father (who in adult life was given the name of Francois but who was normally known as Ah-Seng, and who will be referred to as such in the following) arrived in Seychelles in the early 1920s. It took him a month to get here from his family home in Guangdong by a circuitous route, there being no direct shipping service between Seychelles and China. He disembarked from the first leg of his journey in Calcutta, from where he travelled for three days overland by train to Bombay, followed by a further six-day voyage by sea. As Chow recalls:

> *When my father left in the twenties to seek his fortune abroad, China was in turmoil... After 260 years under the Manchu dynasty, China became a Republic on 1 January 1912. But like Iraq today, and Seychelles in 1976, a declaration does not necessarily make a united country. By the time my father left his home town of Shunde (Suntac), the China he left behind was in virtual civil war led by various warlords.*[44]

That, one assumes, might have been sufficient incentive for his father deciding to leave his homeland. But he also had the advantage of two brothers already living abroad – one in San Francisco and the other in Madagascar – and that would have shown him that migration was possible. Seychelles, however, was not his original choice, as it was the large African island where one of his brothers had settled that he was trying to reach. His arrival in Seychelles was entirely fortuitous, the result of his ship from Bombay having to break its journey *en route* to Madagascar because of an outbreak of a serious disease on board. All the passengers, including his father, were apparently quarantined for six months on Long Island (within view of the main island of Mahé) while the steamer was cleared to carry on its journey. It is not known why he chose to abandon his plan to continue to Madagascar after he completed his period of quarantine, but it proved to be one of those consequential decisions that led to a different future for his family. Paul Chow picks up the story from there:

> *My father's first job in his accidental home away from home, according to our understanding, was as a skilled craftsman in the preparation of dried sea cucumber on one of the outlying islands. He was recruited by Mr Felix Hoareau, the father of Captain Edmond Hoareau. To date, I have no idea which island it was. By the time he took the job, my father had fallen in love with a local girl called Helene Camille from Beau Vallon. According to one of my aunts, the family of four girls and two boys would sometimes go on strolls at the Long Pier chaperoned by their mother, to watch people arrive from the passenger steamers which visited Seychelles once a month. It was on one of those strolls that my father met my mother. It would be interesting to know just how they struck a conversation given the language barrier.*[45]

Marrying a local girl was commonplace in the immigrant community, where most of the new arrivals were single men. But in this case, there was a complication as Paul's father was Buddhist by birth while his mother was Catholic. The Catholic Church did not at the time allow mixed marriages so, when his father got the job on the outlying island, Paul's aunt went to see the parish priest, Father Aloyse, to make the case that her sister would be living in sin if they were not married. Permission was quickly sought from the bishop, who gave his approval. It seems that his mother, though willing to marry, had no intention of moving to the outlying islands.

In all the stories of early immigrants, money was always in short supply so it is surprising to learn that in 1947 Paul's father could afford to take his family to China, to the place of his birth in Guangdong Province. To be fair, he had by then been in Seychelles for more than twenty years and must have lived frugally and put aside savings. At that stage, there were three boys and three girls (with Paul being born after the family returned to Seychelles). It is not known if the intention was to stay permanently in China but, just as it had been when he first left his country, it was still in turmoil. After two years, following the victory of the communist forces over the Nationalist Army, Paul's father escaped with his family to Hong Kong and from there they found their way back to Seychelles, following the same route that he had originally taken. His two elder sons (aged fourteen and fifteen), however, chose to remain in Hong Kong: the eldest never came home – and died in California – while it was forty years before the other son visited Seychelles and was reunited with his family.

Back in Seychelles, Ah-Seng set up a shop and a bakery on his wife's family property in Beau Vallon. And that is how he is remembered by his children, as the village shopkeeper and baker. At the early age of five or six, he used to take Paul with him to Victoria on his regular visits to meet other Chinese immigrants who were all merchants like him: the likes of Mr Sham Peng Tong, Mr Kim Koon, Mr Lai Lam and Mr Lau Tee. Ah-Seng was one of the few immigrant Chinese who could read and write, and on his trips to town he would spend time reading letters and crafting replies for those members of the community who were unable to do so.

In spite of (or perhaps because of) his many business and other activities, he was also a prominent member of the Chinese Association. During Chinese New Year festivals, he would spend days at the pagoda helping to prepare lunch and dinner, and playing mahjong with other Chinese men from all over Seychelles. In those days too, it would not be Chinese New Year if there were no fire crackers and Ah-Seng was one of those who imported them. According to Paul, his father was one of the best Cantonese cuisine cooks in Seychelles. Paul recalls that one day, with his cousins, he caught an eel in the local stream. They were all scared of it but his father was beaming. Soon the eel became a sumptuous Cantonese delicacy. No one, though, had the stomach to eat it, except for Paul and his father. That meant, apart from learning to write the Chinese characters, the young boy also had to attend Chinese cooking lessons, which meant less time to play marbles with his cousins.

Ah-Seng was baptized as a Catholic when Father Tu visited Seychelles from Hong Kong. The occasion was recalled because it was celebrated with a big feast and Paul's job was to help wring the necks of piles of chickens and ducks. The rest of the family was already baptized in the Catholic faith, even before their father himself formally joined as an adult. And, even before his own baptism, he made sure the rest of the family all woke up in good time to make it to mass at Bel Ombre every

Sunday morning. On formally becoming a Catholic, he had to have a Christian name, which is when Francois (evidently after St Francis of Assisi) was added to his Chinese name.

The Chinese language bible was one of the few books Paul saw his father read, apart from a text on Confucius and regular copies of the *Peking Review*. His mother, for her part, could not read or write and – although she could not speak a word of Chinese – she seemed able to understand perfectly almost everything her husband said in Chinese, a feat that Paul still cannot fathom. Sometimes when his father was angry and would shout at him in Chinese, he relied on his mother for the translation.

Because of his scholarly attributes, Ah-Seng became the official agent for certain magazines from China. Two publications which Paul remembers well were *China Pictorial* and *Peking Review*, which were printed in three languages – Chinese, English and French. As a result, their home was regularly visited by the postman on his daily rounds. Mr Elizabeth (the father of Bernard Elizabeth) delivered the parcels and, when he did so, he liked to call in to the shop for a lemonade and cakes, not to mention long conversations with Ah-Seng before returning to Victoria.

The different language versions of *China Pictorial* or *Peking Review* would not always arrive together. Invariably, the English or French version came first and it was Paul's job, though he was still in primary school, to translate into Creole the captions under each of the various photos. He did not attempt the long versions of English text in the *Peking Review* although he did try to read some of it because there was always a copy lying around. When the Chinese language version arrived, his father would remember the translations and would make sure they were corrected in his passable Creole. For Paul, it became a sort of challenge to ensure that he got all of them correct the next time. On reflection, he regards this as the single most important influence in his life, which he thinks created in him an enduring passion for reading.

As the distributor of certain Chinese publications, Ah-Seng was sometimes identified as a communist sympathizer and budding local politicians would pay him a visit. The one who came most often was Mr Harry Hockaday Payet, who launched a party called the Seychelles Archipelago Action Group, and became a good friend. Once, Mr Payet brought a young lawyer to the house. His name was Albert René. James Mancham, too, would come to discuss political ideas. Seychelles at the time was still a colony and the 'China connection' caused some security concerns in the British Army, which one of Paul's brothers had joined in the early 1960s.

In fact, Paul's view is that his father did not have any real affinity with communism and it was probably more a question of nostalgia for the land of his birth. After all, on the eve of communist victory in China, Ah-Seng had fled with his family to Hong Kong and then returned to Seychelles. Paul wondered how much he knew about the starvation of tens of millions of Chinese as a result of Mao's 'Great Leap Forward' policy. He used to say that at that time, in China, 'everybody worked while only one man ate'. Certainly, he had little regard for Mao Tse Tung himself – or, at least, that's what he said. But his Chinese hero was definitely Chou En Lai, the long-suffering Chinese Prime Minister during Mao's rule. He had such reverence for Chou that he named his last son (Paul) after him. It was a source of pride when he told Paul that Chou En Lai was a good man and that his son's name was similar. Chou was the Mandarin way of pronouncing Chow, which was the Cantonese dialect pronunciation; additionally, Paul's Chinese name – Yen Lune – is Cantonese for En Lai.

Ah-Seng died after a long illness, in the year that Paul was admitted to Seychelles College. He was too ill to accompany his son there on his first day, as he had done when the young boy started at St John Bosco Primary six years before. With his passing, one can only speculate how he would have reacted to subsequent events, like the visit of the first senior Chinese officials to Seychelles. But Paul has no doubt that he would have been a proud man today to see what the China he loved had become.

Paul Chow, editor of 'Seychelles Weekly', 2006
Photo courtesy of Paul Chow

Making Good in Paradise

There was little to lure Chinese immigrants to Seychelles in the first place, a remote archipelago under colonial rule, where people had only recently been freed from slavery. There was no gold waiting to be discovered, no promise of easy riches. Any allusion to paradise came much later, a public relations device to attract tourists in the modern era, who would come to experience the white sandy beaches and turquoise sea. That is not what mattered for the small number of Chinese settlers who first arrived on these shores in the latter years of the nineteenth century. For them, paradise was not to be bestowed but earnt; if, as Benjamin Disraeli surmised, 'all Paradise opens' it would not do so on its own.[46]

Even though the pioneer settlers from China wanted to succeed, and were ready to work hard to do so, the means of self-improvement was through small steps. Not everyone would become wealthy or hold an esteemed position in society, but some eventually did. Indeed, for a community with such small numbers overall, there has been a high level of achievement and individuals can be found in various leadership positions. Assuming the total number of people with Chinese ancestry in Seychelles has never risen above one thousand at any one time (and for most of the time well below this figure), one has to ask whether the proportion of 'high achievers' is greater than one might expect. This is not something which can easily be quantified but for such a small community to produce a president and government ministers, successful business leaders and property owners, prominent names in the world of religion and an artist with an international reputation, not to mention individuals who have excelled in medical research and practice, photography and also law, this must at least give pause for thought.

Moreover, one must take into account that few, if any, of the original Chinese immigrants arrived in Seychelles with little more than the clothes they were wearing. There was no capital in the bank to give their various careers a 'kick start', no government agency to fund promising entrepreneurs. For the early generations, only their own labour and invention could take them forward, only their families and friends could help; in other words, people around them with a common sense of determination to make good. It has been very much a collective journey out of poverty. To explain why the Chinese community has done well, it would be facile to suggest that the reason is purely genetic – that there is, somehow, a natural propensity to succeed. All the evidence shows that nothing has come easy and that hard work has been (and remains) a constant theme. Beyond that, one can only speculate, but there do seem to be specific factors which might have contributed to this record of achievement.

First, it is interesting how often one hears of a hunger amongst the pioneers not only to survive but also to improve the conditions for their families. It was, after all, the reason why they had left their homeland in the first place, primarily to escape the clutches of poverty and, once they had escaped it themselves, they wanted to ensure that their children could rise to the next level. Working hard was a constant factor but it is sometimes asked whether this will continue to be so, now that succeeding generations enjoy many advantages that their parents missed. Will they have the same hunger to succeed? Secondly, another important factor is that the family has always been central to Chinese society. The first settlers were often helped by family members who had already established themselves in Mauritius and encouraged relatives to seek new opportunities in Seychelles. And when others followed the example of this small number of pioneers, their first point of contact might then be an uncle or sibling in the Chinese community who would help them to make a start. A third factor is that, although it would be wrong to suggest that business acumen is necessarily a natural trait, it was certainly the outcome of a learning process. Through trial and error, small shops selling basic commodities were opened and different trades pursued. For most migrants these would have been totally new ventures but they learnt what was needed and passed on this experience to their children. In time, too, another factor is the importance attached by parents to education. Even if they, themselves, had not had the same opportunities, they recognized its value to their children. Some things could only be learnt through practice but if there were aspirations to enter professions like law and medicine, then passing exams and going abroad to study was an essential step.

For these (and no doubt other reasons too) the community has cause to be proud of its many achievements. While it is true that the 'hall of fame' is dominated by the names of men, this kind of gender imbalance is typical of most ethnic groups in the past. But this is now changing. That is why, in the following profiles, we are pleased to include the example of a woman of Chinese ancestry who currently holds a leading position as a government minister, and another who represented Seychelles in ambassadorial roles overseas and now occupies a senior post in foreign affairs. It would be remiss, too, if we did not also point to the impressive example of the first woman flight captain for Air Seychelles, Nicole Chang-Leng, who was also the first woman in the airline to fly a Boeing 767. We can point, too, to the outstanding talent of Zoe Chong Seng, who is widely recognized as a rising star in the world of art.

Tales of good fortune

The Chinese symbol for good fortune or good luck

Achievement can be measured in various ways, and the following profiles are by no means exhaustive. One might have included, as well, in this set of profiles, James Chang-Tave, the first Seychellois Roman Catholic priest; Marcel Fayon, co-founder of the country's first photographic shop; and Philip Fock Heng, the first Seychellois to be trained as a pharmacist. As mentioned above, there is also the pilot, Nicole Chang-Leng and the young artist, Zoe Chong Seng.

We have singled out just two business leaders and their families to exemplify this important area of achievement but we could well have included more. Why not, for instance, the Sham Peng Tong family, who might well not have settled in Seychelles at all, but for the fact that their pioneering ancestor disembarked when the boat he was travelling on (bound for Madagascar) needed engine repairs. Since then, the family has not only succeeded in business but retains a strong interest and pride in their Chinese ancestry. As the senior figure in the family, Ah-laye, better known as Laipa, urges his grandchildren to remember their heritage and he enjoys watching Chinese television programmes that show the remarkable development that is ongoing.

In the end, we had to limit our search to a small number of high-achievers to illustrate aspects of the Chinese community, rather than making a claim to be totally comprehensive. Together with those described below, each illustrates something of the wide-ranging contribution made by individuals of Chinese ancestry to the life of Seychelles. Filling some of these gaps to give a more rounded picture of community achievers, might well be something which is later pursued as a cultural activity within the pagoda.

Sir James Mancham

Photo credit: Seychelles News Agency (CC BY)

Known above all as the founding president of the Republic of Seychelles, James R. Mancham was knighted by the British on the eve of the former colony being granted independence. Of Chinese ancestry (family name Man-Cham), his grandfather was the first member of the family to settle in the country. In turn, James's father owned a prospering shipping chandlery and, with extensive property holdings in his portfolio as well, he was able to fund his son's training as a lawyer in London. James was called to the bar in 1961 and returned home in the following year. Always a visionary, he was already thinking of his country's postcolonial future when he formed the Seychelles Democratic Party, which inter alia advocated the retention of close links with Britain.

His contribution to good relations between all classes and ethnicities was warmly acknowledged by the governor of the colony at the time:

> *What pleased me more particularly was that Mr Mancham, the son of Seychellois-Chinese heritage, had been able to achieve so much in the line of communal integration to which I had committed myself on the day that I first set foot in Seychelles. His resolve and inspiration were manifest in the growth of amity, respect and tolerance among the several races of 'these islands of love'.*[47]

None of this was to the liking of his main political opponent, France Albert René, who had formed his own political party with very different aims. For the time being, though, Mancham's party was in the ascendancy and when the British ceded sovereignty to the new republic, he was appointed as the country's first president and duly knighted.

Ousted from the presidency in a coup after just one year, he then spent fifteen years in exile before returning to his homeland in 1992. It was clear on his return that he still enjoyed mass support amongst the people of Seychelles but, instead of trying to force the issue, his message was one of national reconciliation. Party politics had changed during his period of exile and Mancham sensed his time would be better spent in pursuit of peace, not only within his own country but also internationally. It was in that role that he received a number of prestigious awards and lent his name to a research institute for peace and diplomacy at the nation's university. Sir James passed away in 2017.

It is fitting that his son, Alexander, should inherit his father's interest in geopolitics and a commitment to international cooperation. In his role as the UN's Coordination Officer for Mauritius and Seychelles, he looks for ways to support the work of the various United Nations agencies in this part of the western Indian Ocean. At a personal level, he points out that his own Chinese lineage has been diluted because of ancestral intermarriage, but certainly not lost. He has always been attracted to the philosophy of Confucianism and believes that he has inherited typical Chinese values, such as a strong family focus.

Making Good in Paradise

Former family home of the Man-Cham family now Nancum (Southern Village) Kindergarten (Sir James is shown with the kindergarten director at the time)
Photo courtesy of Alex Mancham

Archbishop French Chang Him

Photo by Wang Dongxia

Following a long career serving as an Anglican priest and then Bishop in Seychelles, French Chang Him was appointed Archbishop of the Indian Ocean. In 2014 he was awarded the Order of the British Empire. He comes from a family of ten children – one of whom was killed during the political coup of 1977. Now with the title of Archbishop Emeritus, French Chang Him continues to play an active role in the Anglican Church, as well as supporting a number of charitable organizations.

Archbishop French, as he is popularly known, has never forgotten his Chinese ancestry, which is derived from the lineage of his father, Francis Chang Him; his mother, Amelia, was of mixed African and French descent. Francis left his Cantonese community in Guangdong in the 1920s, with a view to settling in Madagascar but, because of problems with the boat, he was one of those migrants who disembarked at Seychelles instead. He proved to be versatile and was known for a number of skills, including growing vegetables, working as an electrician, repairing watches and then establishing himself as a jeweller. Money could not be wasted and each day he would eat a simple dish of rice mixed with pumpkin and, usually, fish.

French (who, but for an error in the registration process, would have been named, like his father, Francis) recalls as a boy treating the former pagoda as his second home – going there after school to do his homework, reading books in a quiet corner and learning to cook Chinese food in the communal kitchen. There was also an urn, heated with firewood, and, so it seemed, a constant supply of tea. His memories, though, are less about things and more about the emotional attachment to his ancestry.

Archbishop French and his daughter on a visit to China
Photo courtesy of Archbishop French Chang Him

Such emotions were stirred when he made a trip to the village in Guangdong where his father had grown up; it was, understandably, a deeply moving experience. A few years later, in October 2013, he made a second visit to China, this time with his daughter, Frances, as part of a delegation organized by the Chinese Association and led by the late Charlie Ng. Amongst the group were members of the Chinese communities in Mauritius and Madagascar. Together, they laid a plaque to mark the spot where a small group of migrants (his father included) had boarded a river boat to take them to Hong Kong, on the first part of the long journey to their future homes in the Indian Ocean. It was an historic event, sponsored by UNESCO.

Looking ahead, though, the Archbishop worries about the future of the Chinese community in Seychelles and is not yet sure if the Chinese pagoda will be sufficient to stem a steady decline in numbers and the kind of commitment that was evident when he was younger.

Weeling Lee

Weeling Lee with his son Jean
Photo courtesy of Weeling Lee

No discussion of pioneering families who helped to shape the local Chinese community would be complete without recognition of Weeling Lee. Indeed, if there is a doyen of the community it must surely be him. Now, at the grand age of ninety-four, he still remains interested and active in what is going on. When we met him at the home of his youngest daughter, Rose-Mary, and her husband Michael, Mr Lee brought with him a set of publications (all in Mandarin) with highlights of different aspects of the past.

Weeling Lee arrived in Seychelles in 1947, at the age of nineteen, coming from Siping, a Hakka village in Meizhou, Guangdong. At an early age (while still in China), he had been adopted by the Kim Koon family and enjoyed a good education as a boy. As well as Hakka he learnt Mandarin, and later could speak Creole as well. His first job in Victoria was to work with his adoptive parents in their family shop; that helped him to find his way in his new country, but he soon chose to branch out elsewhere. He married Koon Tai Wah, and the couple in due course had five children.

With his experience of working in shops, and with the offer of a loan from the Ah-Moye family of Plaisance, he decided it was time to run his own business. At first, he rented a store in Pointe Conan but in 1964 he showed his characteristic flair and determination by building his own shop in Mont Fleuri. And there it is to this day.

Some of the nearby schools, from where children once came each day to make their purchases, have since closed, but the shop is still a flourishing business and local landmark. What is more, Weeling Lee makes his own daily visit to make sure that everything is running well.

He has always been a busy man but would still find time to contribute to the work of the Chinese Association, in which he was Chairman on different occasions. It gave him great pleasure, too, that Rose-Mary was also elected onto the Executive Committee of the Association, being concerned, like her father, for the good standing of the Chinese community.

The children were encouraged to pursue their higher education outside Seychelles but one of the sons, Jean, chose not to do that. He has always seen Seychelles as his real home and, from his school days, became fully integrated in the multi-cultural society. After several years of working at the Central Bank, he decided that he would have more scope to support local businesses if he set up his own investment company. When asked about his Chinese ancestry, he recalls that, after his mother died, his father took all of the children to the original family village in Meizhou to pay their respects. Jean was fascinated by the experience but has not returned since – though he plans to do so when he has more time to call his own.

Other members of the family have made their own visits to Meizhou, and Weeling Lee has always ensured that their common roots are not forgotten. On such visits, apart from taking with them individual gifts like bicycles and sewing machines, the family has donated valuable infrastructure and a museum for the community. In that way, the link with the past remains strong.

Weeling Lee with his daughter Rose-Mary
Photo by Wang Dongxia

Ambassador Vivianne Fock Tave

Ambassador Fock Tave at a signing ceremony in Beijing, September 2018
Photo courtesy of Vivianne Fock Tave

Presently the Principal Secretary of the Foreign Affairs Department, Vivianne Fock Tave tells a heartwarming story of personal achievement and pride in her Chinese ancestry. She recalls that her father followed the path of his elder brother, from a Cantonese family in a village near Shunde in Guangdong to the distant islands of Seychelles. Still in his teens, he made his own journey in the late-1920s, with little more than the clothes he was wearing. With a typical Chinese propensity to work hard, he first took a job with his brother and was later employed by various shopkeepers in Victoria, and Baie St. Anne, Praslin, until he had saved enough to open his own shop in Bel Ombre.

By then, at the age of thirty-three, he married Agnesina Belle, a Seychellois lady from Takamaka. The couple duly gave birth to a large family of nine children, with the addition of a daughter joining them from a previous relationship. Vivianne was the youngest in the family and describes her parents as loving but also strict. Education was seen as the best way to better themselves, and their parents took a keen interest in their progress at school. When one of her brothers scored 98% in a mathematics exam, he was admonished by his father for not getting full marks. If I were to let two per cent slip in my shop, he said, I would soon be out of business.

The Fock Tave family prior to the birth of Vivianne
Photo courtesy of Vivianne Fock Tave

Most of the children did well at school (Vivianne included) and attended either Seychelles College for boys or the Regina Mundi Convent School for girls. Vivianne next opted to join the National Youth Service and then Seychelles Polytechnic. From there, through a scholarship from the East German government, she chose to study economics at university. After a year at Weimar, learning German, she moved to East Berlin to start her specialism. The falling of the Wall, and the unification of the two halves of the country, led to her restarting her studies (this time in a combined undergraduate/Master's programme) in what was previously West Berlin. Each day she took a train across the old boundary from her home in the former communist bloc to her new university.

On returning to Seychelles in 1996, stimulated by her overseas experience, she obtained a post in Foreign Affairs. In 2010 she achieved her first ambassadorial post, based in Brussels but also accredited to various European countries, as well as the Holy See. But her crowning joy came in 2015, when she was appointed as Ambassador of Seychelles to the People's Republic of China. She had already made a visit to China in 2000 as part of a delegation of African diplomats; now she could take her time to absorb what being there meant to her.

On the first evening of her new assignment, she recalls looking out of her hotel room at the skyline and marvelling at the rate of change that was so evident since her previous visit. It was an emotional moment and her thoughts went immediately to her father and how proud he would have been to have shared the experience. Shortly after, she was even more overwhelmed when she stood before President Xi Jinping, to deliver her letter of accreditation. This was just the start of a memorable period, and her enthusiasm for the new China never waned during her six years as her country's ambassador in Beijing.

Ambassador Bernard Shamlaye

Photo by Wang Dongxia

Bernard Shamlaye (Sham Laye) is a third-generation citizen of Chinese ancestry and the origins of both of his parents can be traced back to Cantonese communities in Guangdong. His mother was born in Seychelles to parents who had been here since the 1920s; in turn, his father arrived later and Bernard's parents married in 1949. Bernard himself comes from a family of six siblings, one of whom (Conrad) is another prominent member of the community.

His father, who owned a small shop on the corner of Royal Street and La Bourdonnais Street, died when Bernard was still at school. As a result, his advancement was due to his natural abilities rather than family wealth. Like his equally talented brother, Conrad, Bernard has contributed in various ways to the modern development of Seychelles. The timing was just right for him as, when independence was declared in the small island state, he had just completed a Master's degree in History and a Postgraduate Diploma in Education. His career then followed a varied and distinguished path in the new regime that led to ministerial and ambassadorial appointments.

Bernard travelled extensively in the course of his work, including to his ancestral homeland. On one visit, he led a delegation to Meizhou and Shunde, in Guangdong Province, and to the Cantonese city of Guangzhou, all in that part of China where most of the migrants who made their way to Seychelles once lived. During the visit, with the help of the authorities, he and Conrad were able to meet some descendants of his father's relatives. On a later occasion, Conrad was taken to the village hall in his father's former community, where he was shown a plaque containing the names of different families, including his own.

With more time on his hands now, Bernard has taken a keen interest in finding out more about Chinese traditions and is attending lessons in Mandarin. While his wife is mainly of African descent and their two sons have married into the wider Seychellois society, he is happy that an interest in Chinese ancestry remains strong in their small community, with visits to the homeland becoming more common. He has shown that it is possible to embrace a multi-ethnic culture without losing touch with one's own roots.

Minister Peggy Vidot

Photo courtesy of Peggy Vidot

As the government minister in charge of the Department of Health (one of the country's toughest challenges), Peggy Vidot has come a long way since she decided at an early age to pursue a career in healthcare. She is well qualified in midwifery, nursing, and health services management and, in addition to extensive experience in different aspects of healthcare in Seychelles, she spent nearly ten years in London as the Health Advisor for the Commonwealth Secretariat. Health is always on the frontline of a nation's concerns but no-one could have anticipated, just a few months into her appointment as minister, that she would be confronted by the pandemic of 2020 and beyond.

With so much going on, the minister still found time to tell us what her Chinese ancestry means to her. Like others we met, she wishes she had found out more about her family background while close relatives and their friends were still alive. What she does recall is that her father (the family name is Wong) arrived in Seychelles when he was just fifteen years old. It seems that he had an uncle who was already here and that was enough to lure him across the ocean. He worked in his uncle's shop and, when he had sufficient experience, he moved to La Digue to run a store by himself. There were only two or three other people of Chinese ancestry on the island but Mr Wong soon found a locally-born wife, and the two of them became parents of twelve children.

Although her father would have had only a rudimentary education – apart from learning French, which he had somehow picked up while still in China, and could write letters in that language – he was determined that his children would seize every opportunity to better themselves. Such was his belief in hard work, supported wholeheartedly by his wife after he died, that all twelve of their offspring (Peggy included) passed the exam for entry to the country's only two grammar schools. Especially coming from the small community in La Digue, this was an outstanding achievement. Sadly, her father passed away when Peggy was only nine, but by then the family had moved back to Mahé.

Although she has little time to spare for personal activities, the minister welcomes the opening of the new pagoda, which she sees as an opportunity to showcase Chinese culture. Her own ancestry is not usually foremost in her thoughts, but it is always there. In a touching recollection, she tells of when she first visited China on official business and of how, when she stepped off the plane, she felt an emotional attachment to the country of her father's birth. It was a sensation that others of Chinese ancestry have clearly felt too.

Dr Conrad Shamlaye

Photo courtesy of Conrad Shamlaye

Like others with Chinese ancestry, Dr Shamlaye's family was Cantonese, coming originally from Guangdong Province. While still at school, he set his sights on becoming a doctor and duly applied for a scholarship to study overseas. Competition was keen but he succeeded in gaining sponsorship for a place in Glasgow to study medicine. Although it was a long way from home, and the cold weather (and the heavy Glaswegian accent of the people he met) was a constant challenge, he took every opportunity to learn from the differences he encountered. In particular, he experienced firsthand the harsh conditions of families in an ailing industrial region living in poverty, which led him to explore the relationship of health to one's surroundings. It was also while he was there that he met his future wife, Heather, who was herself to practice as a doctor when they both left Scotland to settle in Seychelles.

Conrad is a living example of the value of continuous learning when, having passed his professional exams to practice as a doctor, he later obtained postgraduate qualifications in epidemiology and then health economics, both of which he put to good use. Through working in the still-developing health service, he was committed to making a contribution to the improving welfare of the people of Seychelles. It was in the public sector that he took on a number of senior posts in a distinguished career. He was also to hold a variety of honorary positions in organizations in Seychelles (including the Red Cross Society, of which he was a founder member) and with international bodies like the World Health Organization (where he served on the Executive Board).

As well as being a caring practitioner and a very able administrator, he rightly gained international recognition for his research, not least of all for his long-term, collaborative study of the possible effects of a fish diet on children's health. It was questioned whether exposure to higher-than-average levels of mercury would affect child development. With fellow researchers at the University of Rochester in the US – subsequently widening the network to include centres in Sweden, Northern Ireland and Switzerland – Dr Shamlaye has remained at the heart of the study for more than thirty years. As another example, through his contacts in the World Health organization, a further international project was started, focusing this time on the incidence and effects of intestinal parasites amongst schoolchildren. As well as benefiting the research population, it also led to wider benefits for the families of affected children.

Making Good in Paradise

Conrad Shamlaye with family members during a visit to his home community
Photo courtesy of Conrad Shamlaye

George Camille

Photo by Wang Dongxia

George is in the third generation of a Cantonese family who, like others in the community, came to Seychelles in search of a better life. His father, Ahloye, was a baker who owned a small shop in La Digue.

George did well at school and won a scholarship to study art in London. But politics in the one-party state at home intervened and, when he returned to Seychelles, he soon discovered that he would not be accepted for a job in the public sector. This was probably the best thing that could have happened to him as he turned, instead, to a freelance career in art. At the age of 24 he established Sunstroke Studio, and the rest is history. From a single building, new studios have been added to cater for his diverse activities and to offer opportunities for young artists too. Fine art, etchings, sculpture and printing are amongst the varied techniques in his ever-expanding portfolio. With his English wife, Jayne, he moves just as easily across geographical boundaries as in various aspects of art, and he exhibits in many countries. His Chinese ancestry is an important part of him – he is an active member of the Chinese Association – but his interests and reputation are truly international.

Seybrew Time, an example of the art of George Camille
Courtesy of George Camille

As well as the Sunstroke Studio, George's work can be seen at two galleries, one in what was a traditional house (which he restored himself) in Victoria and one on La Digue. His art makes an immediate impression and one is drawn beyond the bold colours to his thought-provoking images. He is an advocate of culture in the broadest sense and has directly influenced the completion of the new Chinese pagoda. The presence of a shop in the pagoda, displaying works by various artists, is his brainchild and it is already bringing in a steady number of visitors.

Joseph Kim Koon

Photo courtesy of the Kim Koon family

Another pioneering family is that of Joseph Kim Koon. Over the best part of a century, the Kim Koon family has exemplified the business acumen and success of Chinese traders. Joseph, who left Guangdong in the 1920s, joined his father in Seychelles, and subsequently established the family business. The family has owned an old colonial style shop in Market Street, in the heart of Victoria, since 1956. Starting as general merchants, the business diversified into a bakery, soap production and, later, electronics and motor vehicles.

At one point, Joseph sent his children to China, in the belief that it could offer a better future for them, but with the advent of communism in 1949 he quickly brought them back. He was father to no fewer than nineteen offspring and lived to see five generations grow up in his adopted country. A number of them have visited China to trace their roots but Seychelles remains their home. Joseph, himself, died in 2002.

The founding president, James Mancham, recalled in 2014 that the Kim Koons were part of a community of 'prominent players in the sphere of commerce and trading' but by then 'lost in the mist of the past':

> *... the names of such noteworthy Seychellois-Chinese as Affoy, Ah-Cheen, Ah-Kong, Ah-Lock, Ah-Shung, Ah-Weng, Chang Lai-Seng, Chang-Leng, Chang-Sam, Chang Tak Hue, Chang-Tive, Chong-Seng, Chow, Chung-Faye, Chung-Loye, Fayon, Hissen, Kim Koon, Lai-Hue, Lai-Lam, Leong Kee, Leong Pon, Low-Nam, Low-Tee, Pon-Waye... Even today we have such personalities as Shamlaye, Fock-Tave, Weeling among others who are serving under the banner of the Third Republic.*[48]

Kim Koon with family and friends at the opening of his new shop in Victoria in 1956
Photo courtesy of Robert Chong Seng

Dr Guy Ah-Moye

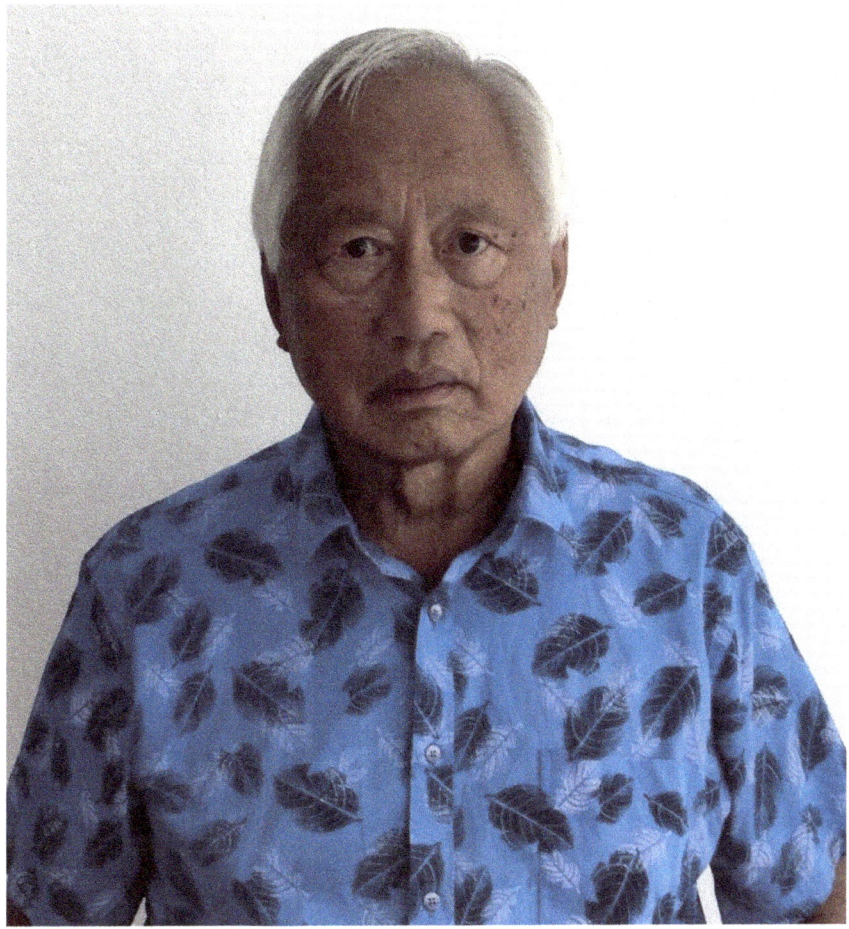

Photo courtesy of Guy Ah-Moye

When asked about his Chinese ancestry, Dr Ah-Moye is proud to tell of his Hakka lineage. The Hakka, he will explain, were 'guest workers' and showed resilience in adapting to new environments, as his own career in medicine has borne out.

With the help of a Commonwealth scholarship, he was able to study medicine at St Bartholomew's Medical School (popularly known as Barts), one of the leading teaching hospitals in London. After he qualified in 1966, he remained in the UK for several years until he became a Member of the Royal College of Physicians. At that point he returned to Seychelles, ready to help in building the health service in what was still a British colony. He made a quick impression when in charge of all medical inpatients, and he took a lead in introducing a family planning programme. In turn, he served as the Acting Chief Medical Officer for the country, where he was closely involved in designing and implementing the country's first five-year medical plan.

Over the best part of a decade, he made an important contribution to his, by then, newly-independent country. But he was uneasy with the direction of the single-party state, so in 1979 he returned to the UK. And there he remained, combining medical practice with a successful business as Senior Medical Director of an enterprise with the acronym SELDOC, until he finally retired in 2012. At that point he returned to Seychelles.

In recent years, Dr Ah-Moye has shared his experience in the field through teaching interns and nurses, through various committee appointments, and through his writing and advice on various issues. He has never forgotten his ancestral homeland, taking the opportunity to visit his father's village and to travel widely in China. The now-completed pagoda has been a focus of recent attention and his enthusiasm to see it used as a cultural centre has supported and inspired others.

At the birthplace of Chairman Mao in Shaoshan, Hunan Province
Photo courtesy of Guy Ah-Moye

Charlie Ng Ping Cheun

Photo by Wang Dongxia

Charlie left the Chinese community in Mauritius in 1982, to come to Seychelles as one of a number of teachers recruited by the Ministry of Education. He could offer vocational skills and was appointed to a post in the then Seychelles Technical School in Mont Fleuri. From there, he later moved to the new Seychelles Polytechnic at Anse Royale, where he worked for the next twelve years, until leaving teaching for the private sector. First, he joined an electronics firm, and then he set up his own shop in Orion Mall, selling electrical and electronic goods.

Charlie's Chinese ancestry dates back to migrants from Guangdong who settled in Mauritius in the nineteenth century, his extended family remaining there after Charlie left for Seychelles. Soon after arriving in Victoria, he married Anne Ah-Weng and the couple gave birth to three sons. In 1995, Charlie was given Seychelles citizenship. Like so many of his counterparts, he combined his new Seychelles identity with a continuing pride in his ancestry. Recognizing the latter, he was active in the Chinese Association and was for several years its enthusiastic

Chairman; it was, in fact, during his tenure that he saw the start of the present pagoda project and spent many hours helping to raise the initial capital and appointing building contractors.

In spite of the time spent on the project, and his commitment to making a success of his shop, Charlie was always active on a number of other fronts too. He played table tennis, badminton and, his first love, tennis, becoming in due course President of the Seychelles Tennis Association. As a local businessman, he was elected on three occasions to be President of the Rotary Club. Somehow, he also found time to attend classes of the Confucius Institute, where he excelled as a student learning Mandarin. The fact is that Charlie was the kind of person who always wanted to help his community, whether it be people who shared his ancestral background or in the community at large. In turn, he was well known and liked throughout Seychelles. It came as a shock then, while this research was nearing completion, to learn of his sudden and unexpected passing. We have all lost a dear friend and a role model of an ethnically diverse society. He would have welcomed this story of the community that meant so much to him personally, and we, in turn, honour his memory.

Robert Chong Seng

Photo by Wang Dongxia

Robert Chong Seng presently chairs the Chinese Association. His life story typifies the very essence of the Chinese community, a mix of respect for tradition but also an ambition to branch out and chart his own future. His father came to Seychelles in the 1950s, from a village near Meizhou in Guangdong province. Although, as a new migrant, he had always spoken Hakka, he was offered a job by the businessman, Kim Koon, and quickly learnt French and English. This aptitude for languages caught the attention of his employer, and he was soon asked to write letters for the company. Unfortunately, his father died when Robert was just eighteen months old. Together with three siblings, Robert was brought up by his hard-working mother who, fortunately, had inherited a small shop. She was always proud of her children, who were all to graduate from UK universities; Robert himself was awarded an MBA from the University of Surrey.

It was not an easy start in life and, to add to it all, he was bullied at school for being Chinese. What he remembers most of his childhood, though, is the long hours spent helping his mother in the family shop. He found it boring but made the most of it and, while his friends played outside, he sat in a corner and taught himself to play the guitar. From that early experience, he vowed that he would never be a shopkeeper. Instead, he wanted a professional career and qualified as an aeronautical engineer, which led, first, to him working in that capacity for Air Seychelles, before extending his skills to executive management; in all, he worked for the national airline for a total of forty years. On retiring, he devoted himself to playing an active part in the ambitious project to replace the original pagoda that had been demolished in 2014. A succession of obstacles had to be overcome and it was only in 2022 that the new building, finally cleared of outstanding debts and bank charges, could be opened to the community.

Robert's energy is boundless and, when asked to reveal the secret of his youthfulness, he explains that he keeps himself stimulated by learning new skills every day, and by playing several musical instruments. He is an example to us all.

Community Perspectives

Through our various interviews and written records, we can see how the Chinese community in Seychelles views its ties with its former homeland. It is a mixed response, with a difference between those families that have been in Seychelles for several generations and those who are relative newcomers. Amongst the former is a real sense of integration and identity with their present homeland, combined with an enduring attachment to the traditions and culture of their heritage. Of those who arrived more recently, their ties with China remain strong and they speak to each other in Mandarin. Their interest in Seychelles is limited to its business opportunities, and they have few contacts outside their own group.

But how, in turn, does China regard such diverse communities? Of course, Seychelles is one of the smallest of its kind, but for China the diaspora as a whole is a different matter. With a total population across the world approaching sixty million, the Chinese diaspora is a source of potential influence and value in its global transactions. In the rest of this chapter, we offer a sense of this wider picture, a global view from our study that embraces even the small island state of Seychelles; the latter is a small piece in the jig-saw but without it the picture would be incomplete.

'Guides, go-betweens and participants'

Officials have started to see the diaspora not only as a key conduit for high-end technology through involvement in Chinese-led multi-national technology development initiatives, but also as a way to realize broader geo-economic ambitions.[49]

Given his vision of China as a global power, it is not surprising that a lead in recognizing the importance of the diaspora was taken by Xi Jinping; this was initiated in 1995, before he assumed the presidency, when he was party secretary in Fujian. It was then that he advocated a policy of 'big overseas Chinese work', urging greater cooperation between modern China and the diaspora. His ideas took shape and by the time he became president, they had become a central part of the 'Chinese dream'. Economic modernization, technological innovation and cultural revival could all be rolled into one in the new strategy, taking China beyond the restrictive interests of regions and institutions.[50]

This recognition of the importance of the diaspora is founded on an understanding that the bonds of Chinese ancestry are not easily broken. Even several generations after leaving their homeland, families will piece together the stories of their unique heritage. They may well have become closely integrated in societies far from China, a process often strengthened through local marriage, but they are still in their hearts Chinese. One's roots run deep and this is at the heart of the strategic initiative to embrace far-flung communities. Numbers alone cannot necessarily be translated into political support; not everyone will be comfortable with communist rule but the cultural affinity to be found in the diaspora crosses ideological boundaries.

There are as many as fifteen million migrants who left China after the introduction of reforms, seeking new business opportunities around the world. These settlers have been termed the 'new migrants' and are described as 'highly educated, wealthy, and willing to forge close relations with mainland China'.[51] In fact, observation suggests that this elite group is matched by younger migrants who are ambitious and energetic but still have to succeed in their various vocations. Understandably, amongst both groups of newcomers, links with the homeland are still fresh and there is a natural commitment to further those interests. There is common pride in what the modern state of China is achieving.

In their different ways, new and more recent members of the diaspora retain a strong attachment to their Chinese ancestry. Especially for families who have settled in a country like Seychelles for several generations, nothing counts for more than the opportunity to make a visit to their ancestral homeland. As part of the overall strategy to strengthen support amongst the diaspora, known as *qiaowu*, is a specific programme of 'root seeking' tours for overseas Chinese:

> *The tours are directed towards foreign nationals of Chinese descent who want to understand the homeland of their ancestors. The tours involve visiting the participants' ancestral villages, and rebuilding ancestral halls.*[52]

The tours (which are heavily subsidized) have attracted an estimated 400,000 and are especially popular with young people. Additionally, reference has been made in an earlier chapter to individuals in Seychelles who have made their own arrangements to trace their ancestral background. Distant relatives have been contacted and shrines visited where the family name evokes deep-seated emotions. In spite of the passing of time, over several generations, and the adoption of new lifestyles as well as citizenship, it seems that the pull to the past remains unbroken.

Meanwhile, in addition to trips to the homeland, the Confucius Institute is a familiar part of life in diaspora communities. The Confucius initiative is designed, especially, to introduce other ethnicities to the traditions and culture of China, past and present. No less important, it also gives local Chinese communities an opportunity to renew, or in many cases experience for the first time, familiarity with ancestral celebrations and pursuits. Activities in a typical programme might range from calligraphy to tai chi, and from language classes in Mandarin to cuisine. In Seychelles, the new pagoda offers an obvious home for this kind of programme.

(Above) *Tai Chi class at the new pagoda / Chinese Cultural Centre*
(Below) *Chinese language class*
Photos by Qiao Dejian

Home and homeland

The Asia-Pacific is our shared home.[53]

On one of the steep slopes overlooking Victoria (in the district known as St Louis) is the embassy which marks China's official presence in Seychelles, an important part of the diplomatic landscape. Indeed, when the former colony in 1976 celebrated its independent status, China was one of the first nations to recognize the new nation. On reflection, one can see why it made this early move.

Although China had not at that stage formalized its pro-Africa policy, it could see the ideological implications of the post-colonial changes that were sweeping that continent. After years of subjugation by European powers, the newly-independent nations were eager to break with the past and embrace a more egalitarian approach. Following a coup in Seychelles in 1977, which saw the removal of the founding president and his pro-British stance, the small island state proved to be a case in point. Under the leadership of the new president, France Albert René, the country committed itself to a socialist future. With the Cold War by then at its height, Seychelles was naturally drawn into the Soviet bloc. This alignment was never in doubt although René, where he could see benefits, deftly managed at the same time to retain links with the United States and other Western nations. China took an early opportunity to build its own embassy and was joined in the capital by other regimes in the same political bloc, notably the Soviet Union, Cuba and Libya. North Korea did not have its own presence but the communist state was favoured in various ways by President René.[54] As well as these official residencies, visiting delegations were regularly welcomed from other socialist countries, especially from Eastern Europe and different parts of Africa which embraced socialism. Messages of friendship were exchanged and scholarships were provided for Seychellois students to attend universities in those countries.

Ideology apart, the question is sometimes asked why China, a powerful nation with a population rivalled only by that of India, values a close relationship with one of the world's smallest states. The answer has more to do with location than size. China traditionally takes a long-term view and it will not have missed the fact that these islands in the western Indian Ocean could offer landing points in an otherwise remote part of the world, *en route* to Africa. Victoria itself has a deep-water port that lends itself to facilities for refuelling and light repairs. More than that, Seychelles is strategically placed in relation to trade routes that are vital to China's own interests. Across the north of the ocean, east-west shipping lanes connect the Suez Canal and the oil-rich states in the Middle East with the major Asian markets and producers; while busy north-south routes lead to and from the southern tip of Africa and the Atlantic, passing close to the Seychelles archipelago.

The relationship has, in fact, been beneficial for both countries and in June 2021, to mark its 45th anniversary, the many achievements over that period were duly acknowledged. In the words of the Chinese Ambassador, H.E. Guo Wei:

Over the past 45 years, the two countries have always treated each other as equals and the bilateral relations have enjoyed a sound momentum of growth, setting a good example of sincere friendship, solidarity, cooperation, mutual benefit and win-win outcomes between countries.[55]

Ambassador, H.E. Guo Wei
Picture courtesy of the Chinese Embassy in Seychelles

A subsequent report listed some of the many direct benefits enjoyed by Seychelles:

> ... *in various sectors, including education, agriculture, health, housing, and infrastructure as well as fisheries and environment. China has built some landmark infrastructure in Seychelles including the parliament building, the Palais de Justice, housing projects, Anse Royale hospital. Still ongoing is a new headquarters for Seychelles Broadcasting Corporation, funded by the Chinese government. Furthermore, over 1,600 Seychellois have undergone short or long training courses in Chinese institutions and nearly 200 on Chinese-government scholarships. A Chinese medical team and volunteers have also served in Seychelles for decades. As for trade, Ambassador Guo Wei said that trade between the two countries had grown steadily over the past decades, reaching a record in 2019.*[56]

In return, there has been a tacit understanding that Seychelles would lend its support to China as a friend from Africa in the international arena. The relationship between the two nations has worked well and the difference in size has not been an issue. Small though Seychelles is, its sovereignty has always been respected by the larger nation. A measure of this is that Seychelles remains free to interact with countries of different political persuasions. New ambassadors present their credentials to the President of Seychelles and government ministers are in regular contact with the Chinese Embassy when there are issues of common interest.

In contrast, members of the Chinese community have limited contact on a day-to-day basis with their embassy. Victoria is a small capital but the Chinese community and the official world of the embassy operate in largely separate circles. This is not a question of exclusion, so much as respecting their different spheres of influence. From time to time, however, it is to the advantage of both parties to make an exception, as was the case when the Chinese Association called for financial support to enable the completion of the present pagoda.

Another example is the annual China-Seychelles Festival, which coincides with the Chinese New Year celebrations. This brings different groups together, not only members of the local community and officials from the embassy but also representatives of the Seychelles government. It is a time to showcase Chinese culture and the embassy will usually arrange for visiting dancers or singers to demonstrate their artistic skills. China's distinctive cuisine is also a feature and popular delicacies are readily available.

Dance Troupe at Seychelles-China Day celebrations
Photo courtesy of the Chinese Embassy in Seychelles

In the words of a former Chinese ambassador:

> *First held in 2014, the Seychelles-China Day has become a significant platform for people-to-people and cultural exchanges between our two countries, and effectively strengthened our mutual understanding and friendship. The opening of the China Day indicates the up-coming Chinese Spring Festival, which is the grandest festival in China… During the Spring Festival, every household will stick red couplets on the doors, hang up red lanterns, post lucky words, set off fireworks, watch the Spring Festival Gala and visit relatives and friends. Chinese children will receive lucky money in a red packet (called hongbao),*

which is the most exciting moment of the year for them. Nowadays, sending the digital red packets is a popular way to greet relatives and friends during the Chinese New Year. [57]

Spring Festival celebrations
Photo courtesy of the Chinese Embassy in Seychelles

Although celebratory events were stalled during the coronavirus pandemic, a pattern of contact with the community has been established. China will be satisfied that it has another friend in the region while, for Seychelles, good relations with China represent an important part of its own place in the Indian Ocean. Small island states have to be adept in navigating international waters and, while valuing their own sovereignty, they need to foster good relations with other countries, especially the major powers. The vibrancy and loyalty of the Chinese community in Seychelles is one way to make this happen.

Epilogue

Our modest project, designed to tell the story of the Chinese community in Seychelles, coincided with the completion of the new pagoda in the centre of Victoria. While we filled the remaining gaps in our research, on the ground the final touches were applied to the emergent building. We could hardly ignore the symbolism of this juxtaposition; indeed, it was to have a profound influence on how we concluded our own thoughts.

The new pagoda on the evening of its opening
Photo by Qiao Dejian

As we stood at the edge of the busy market and looked across the narrow lane towards the new building, it seemed that we were left with some unresolved questions. Should we be interpreting the completion of the pagoda as a sign of the past or the future? Does it represent the culmination of a hitherto unbroken chain of events that started with the arrival on these shores of a lone migrant in 1863? Was this merely further evidence of the community's resilience, ingenuity and continuity? Or should we see the building before us, instead, as the start of something different? Were we witnessing the end of one phase of development or the beginning of another? And, most tellingly, what does the future hold for the Chinese community?

Why, one might ask, should we even allow any doubt to creep into our conclusion? After all, the story we have told of the community in history is one with which all those with Chinese ancestry should be proud. Moreover, across Seychelles the community continues to be held in high regard. And deservedly so. As we have shown, although numbers have remained small, their contribution to this island nation as a whole has been valued. The roll of honour includes eminent politicians and professionals in different fields, religious luminaries and talented individuals in the arts, not to mention successful business leaders and industrious traders. Meanwhile, out of the limelight, others in the community went quietly about their lives, each helping to knit society together in their own way. They exemplified the value of a sound family life, they gained a reputation for their hard work, and they proved to be good neighbours. Moreover, no-one could reasonably question the extent of their integration and loyalty to Seychelles. Thus, we see numerous examples of inter-marriage, of children who mixed well in multi-ethnic schools, and a commitment to work for the nation as a whole. Time and again, we were told in our research that men and women of Chinese ancestry, whose families can be counted through several generations, regard themselves first and foremost as Seychellois. Not that they have ever forgotten their antecedent culture; there has always been a harmonious balance between the two.

So, to ask the question again, why are we left with a nagging doubt that the community might not be in as sound a position as the imposing appearance of the pagoda would suggest? Does this fine new building symbolize the solidity of the community it will serve? Or are we correct to end with a note of caution?

Our qualified response has more to do with demographics and a wider picture of global change than with local history. The first generations had every reason to stay close to each other, finding comfort and support in the presence of fellow migrants who shared the same culture and aspirations. A background of poverty and the desire to escape it was the unifying force that bound them together. In time, though, this need for interdependence lessened and, while a sense of Chinese ancestry remained deeply embedded, they also led the lives of Seychellois citizens. They maintained an active Chinese Association but that would become less a means of survival in an alien country, and more an opportunity to recall traditions and nourish a shared culture. Many of its members prospered and the building of the new pagoda itself was made possible through their generosity of spirit, shown in a willingness to make loans and donations as well as pooling their invaluable business acumen. It was undoubtedly a successful project, achieving what it set out to do. And yet, as we sensed in some of our interviews and in our own perceptions, there is also a sense of uneasiness.

For one thing (even allowing for early rivalries between Cantonese and Hakka), everyone we spoke to recognized that there was no longer the same degree of purpose within the community as there had been in the past. Alongside those who now see themselves as Seychellois with Chinese ancestry, new cohorts have arrived who remain steadfastly Chinese nationals. These more recent arrivals show less interest in tradition and more in the business opportunities that attracted them to this part of the world. They are, in many ways, indistinguishable from other groups of 'expats', here to do a job and then leave. The situation may change if they decide to settle permanently in Seychelles, but that is how it is now.

More fundamental to the future of the community is the simple fact that younger generations are unlikely to inherit the same sense of commitment to their Chinese ancestry as that of their parents and grandparents. They have grown up in families with mixed marriages, they attended multi-ethnic schools and made friends from a variety of backgrounds. Like young people everywhere, they will now regard themselves as global citizens. In contrast with previous generations, their boundaries are no longer confined to a small cluster of streets in Victoria; to coin a phrase, the world is now their oyster. All of this is, in many ways, a laudable trend in terms of barriers falling away and the encouragement of ethnic harmony. Undeniably, though, it leads young people away from the clearly marked paths followed by their ancestors, for whom Chinese traditions and family life carried more weight. 'Community' has acquired a new meaning for succeeding generations.

None of the above means that the Chinese community will necessarily be unable to withstand these changes. In spite of countervailing pressures, beliefs in a shared ancestry remain strong and the community is hardly likely to wither away. We can point to scenarios, but that is all they are; the future is beyond our ability to predict. It is not impossible, of course, that the recent cohorts of 'expat' immigrants will choose to make Seychelles their home and take pride in joint loyalties, just as their long-established neighbours with Chinese ancestry have done. Nor is it impossible that young descendants of families who regard themselves as Seychellois will choose to assert their own Chinese identity, using social media to connect with the many branches of the world-wide diaspora. They may see themselves as champions of modern China, inspired by and proud to be part of the rapid transition to world power status. China's continuing economic development will offer opportunities for all who can claim a common ancestry (no matter how distant it might now have become). For today's young pioneers, the boundaries of the global Chinese community are limitless.

All of this is conjecture but not beyond the bounds of possibility. We use the pagoda as a symbol of what might change. Its custodians are faced with a challenge, to make it meaningful for the twenty-first century. When one thinks of the difficulties confronted by the impoverished migrants who first came to these shores, and the obstacles they overcame, this new challenge is entirely manageable. It will require the kind of persistence and invention that has been seen before. But the alternative – the spectre of an empty pagoda, reflecting the dissolution of the community it serves – simply cannot be contemplated.

It will be recalled that at the outset of this project we shared our belief that public opinion cannot be shaped by geopolitics alone – whether under the banners of continents or blocs. Human society is more finely textured and it is not enough to corral everyone into one alignment or another. That is why, although we have acknowledged broader trends of history and politics, we have focused on the realm of individuals and community. This is where we could see what people are really like and how well they have integrated in their adoptive homeland. Their story gives pause for hope in the future. It gives us grounds to answer our own questions.

Thus, we conclude that the Chinese community will not be as tight-knit in the future as in the past. Ties have already loosened. Globalization has set a new context. But locality will remain important. Finding the right balance between the two represents the biggest challenge for the community in Seychelles. Perhaps the pagoda itself – formally named the Seychelles Chinese Cultural Centre – will be the venue for discussions about getting the balance right. There could hardly be a more a fitting place to shape a new agenda. And it is certainly not beyond the wit of this remarkable community to find answers.

As a final word on the inevitability of change – not as a linear process but as a cycle – what better than to draw on a Chinese saying?

> *Falling leaves settle on their roots.*
> *Everything reverts to its original sources.*

The end might, indeed, be just the beginning.

Cutting the ribbon at the opening ceremony of the new pagoda, 26 June 2022
Photo by Qiao Dejian

A Personal Reflection by Wang Dongxia

It's like walking on the beach and picking up a few shells that were hit by the wind and waves. This small book only briefly describes and reflects the Chinese history of Seychelles from one side. In the context of different eras, the inextricably linked ways of overseas Chinese and China have never been interrupted. Chinese traditions and culture have always had a certain vitality in this island country in the Indian Ocean. Generations of overseas Chinese have played an active role in making a better life and a harmonious society. Peace, cooperation, harmony and development are the common aspirations of human beings and are the aspirations of a small Chinese community who have been fighting silently for a long time. The successful completion of the new Seychelles Chinese Cultural Centre bears witness to the aspirations for a better life.

A common research interest in this community is the basis for my collaboration with Professor Dennis Hardy. During the research process, we experienced a friendly, cooperative and family-informative attitude to the older generation of overseas Chinese and their descendants through direct contact with them. I am moved by this, and I am also gratified by the current living conditions and achievements of these Seychellois Chinese. The world is diverse. In the rich ocean of human civilization, there are countless beautiful shells, showing different brilliance in the course of history. It is hoped that the existence of the Chinese community in Seychelles today can reflect the life trajectory and real state of most of the older generation of Chinese people. There is a saying in China: *The place where my heart stays is my hometown.* I wish for all overseas Chinese to live in harmony and be happy.

Wang Dongxia

Notes and References

1. 'The overseas Chinese: a long history'. *The UNESCO Courier*, 2021 (4).
   https://en.unesco.org/courier/2021-4/overseas-chinese-long-history#:~:text=There%20are%20more%20than%2010.7,Organization%20for%20Migration%20(IOM%20)
2. John Kean, 'China's galaxy empire'. *Eurozine*, 17 March 2021. https://www.eurozine.com/chinas-galaxy-empire/
3. Toh, Han Shih (2017). *Is China an Empire?* Singapore: World Scientific, p.13.
4. For instance, see Judith van de Looy, 'Africa and China: A Strategic Partnership?', ASC Working Paper 67/2006. African Studies Centre, Leiden, The Netherlands.
5. Bernard Z. Keo and Nathan D. Gardner, 'Made in China or born abroad? Creating identity and belonging in the Chinese Diaspora'. *Association for Asian Studies*, Vol. 25:2, Fall 2020.
6. Su Zhou, 'Number of Chinese immigrants in Africa rapidly increasing'. *China Daily*, 14 January 2017. http://www.chinadaily.com.cn/world/2017-01/14/content_27952426.htm]
7. *Ibid*.
8. Allegedly a quote by Woody Allen.
9. Michelle Locke, 'Sounds, smells, color converge in Chinatown'. *The Olympian*, 30 January 2011.
   https://www.theolympian.com/living/travel/article25281736.html
10. Zhuang Guotu, 'The overseas Chinese: a long history'. The UNESCO Courier, 2021 (4).
    https://en.unesco.org/courier/2021-4/overseas-chinese-long-history
11. Patrick Mendis (2013). *Peaceful War: How the Chinese Dream and the American Destiny Create a Pacific New World Order*. Lanham, Maryland: Rowman and Littlefield International.

12. Information on Zheng He's visits to Africa has been derived from unpublished notes by the Seychelles historian, Julian Durup, and from entries in *Encyclopaedia Britannica and the Geographical Magazine*.
13. President Xi Jinping, 'Opening speech at the Roundtable Summit of the Belt and Road Forum for International Cooperation', 15 May 2017. https://www.ilsole24ore.com/art/excerpts-of-president-xi-jinping-s-quotable-quotes-on-the-belt-and-road-initiative-AB6JdEgB?refresh_ce=1
14. From a speech at Nazarbayev University, Astana, Kazakhstan, 7 September 2013.
15. Xi Jinping was appointed General Secretary of the Communist Party in November 2012.
16. Ella Wheeler Wilcox, 'The Winds of Fate'. *Poems of Optimism*, 1919.
17. Logan Pauley and Hamza Shad, *op.cit.*
18. Amy McDonald, 'A bitter look at the sweet history of brown sugar'. *David M. Rubenstein Rare Book & Manuscript Library at Duke University*, 25 February 2016. https://blogs.library.duke.edu/rubenstein/2016/02/25/amari-stokes/
19. Rashila Vigneshwari Ramchurn, 'Life on sugar estates in colonial Mauritius'. *Journal of Anthropology and Archaeology*, December 2018, Vol. 6, No. 2.
20. Huguette Li-Tio-Fane Pineo (1985). *Chinese Diaspora in Western Indian Ocean*. Mauritius: Editions de l'Océan Indien and Chinese Catholic Mission (English edition).
21. *Ibid*, p.3.
22. *Ibid*, p.122.
23. *Ibid*, pp.117-118.
24. Federica Guccini and Mingyuan Zhang, 'Being Chinese in Mauritius and Madagascar: comparing Chinese diasporic communities in the western Indian Ocean'. *Journal of Indian Ocean World Studies*, 2021, Vol.4, No.2, p.96.
25. Extract from a quote by Franklin D. Roosevelt.

26 Sharon Ernesta, '6 ways the Chinese helped shape Seychelles'. Seychelles News Agency, 20 February 2020. http://www.seychellesnewsagency.com/articles/12408/+ways+the+Chinese+helped+shape+Seychelles

27 Burton Benedict, 'Family firms and economic development'. *Southwestern Journal of Anthropology*, Vol. 24, No. 1 (Spring, 1968), pp.1-19.

28 *Ibid*.

29 Kuczynski R.R. (1949) *Demographic Survey of the British Empire*, London, 1949, vol. II, p. 925.

30 'Early Chinese in the Seychelles: marriages, births and deaths'. A draft note by Julian Durup.

31 This reference (translated into English by Mrs Wang Donxia) is extracted from a description of characteristics of Chinese migrants in Africa: 非洲侨情及其特点; 朱慧玲;《八桂侨刊》年第一期

32 Reproduced in English, in Gilles Gerard, *Les Seychellois d'Origine Chinoise: Approche anthropologique des phénomènes acculturation dans une société creole.* Université de la Réunion, October 1992, p.37.

33 Sharon Ernesta, 'The man who brought great Chinese cuisine to Seychelles is remembered'. *Seychelles News Agency*, 31 July 2021.

34 Gilles Gerard, *Les Seychellois d'Origine Chinoise: Approche anthropologique des phénomènes acculturation dans une société creole.* Université de la Réunion, October 1992.

35 *Ibid*.

36 The extract appears to be from a handbook of the Chinese Association, dated 1928.

37 Gerard, *op.cit.*

38 Chinese Association of Seychelles. https://findsun.net/p-7681732/chinese-association-of-seychelles

39 The response of one interviewee, a third-generation resident.

40 Given the constraints of the exercise – especially the absence of an agreed database for the Chinese population – it is inevitable that the selection of interviewees could not be undertaken on a fully scientific basis. But in trying to achieve a representative sample, it is hoped that common sense and a knowledge of the community – taken alongside separate interviews of with community leaders (in the following section) – has resulted in a reasonably reliable cross-section of 'China in Seychelles'.

41 Nicole Constable, ed. (1996). *Guest People: Hakka identity in China and abroad.* Seattle: University of Washington Press.

42 Horace Walpole, who in 1754 is believed to have coined the term, 'serendipity'.

43 This account is based on an article in Seychelles Weekly, 9 February 2007, written by the editor of the newspaper, Paul Chow. Through this publication, Mr Chow expressed his opposition to the majority party (and for fifteen years the only party) until the balance changed in 2020.

44 *Ibid.*

45 *Ibid.*

46 Benjamin Disraeli (1831). *The Young Duke.*

47 James Mancham, 'Letter to the Editor: Seychelles-China-Day Celebrations'. *The Nation*, February 2014.

48 *Ibid.*

49 Timothy Heath, 'Beijing's influence operations target Chinese diaspora', 1 March 2018. https://warontherocks.com/2018/03/beijings-influence-operations-target-chinese-diaspora/

50 Hong Liu, 'Opportunities and anxieties for the Chinese diaspora in Southeast Asia'. Current History, Vol. 115, No. 784, November 2016, pp.312-318.

51 Zhuang Guotu, a scholar at Xiamen University, in Heath, op.cit.

52 Almén, Oscar (2020). *The Chinese Communist Party and the Diaspora.* Stockholm: FOI (Swedish Defence Research Agency).

53 Xi Jinping, 2020.

54   As well as appointing his own North Korean guards, René made a number of visits to Pyongyang.
55   Patsy Athanase, 'Seychelles, China celebrates 45 years of diplomatic ties'. *Seychelles News Agency*, 26 June 2021.
56   *Ibid*.
57   Vidya Gappy, 'Seychelles-China Day set for January 17 & 18'. *The Nation*, 9 January 2020.

www.ingramcontent.com/pod-product-compliance
Lightning Source LLC
Chambersburg PA
CBHW042130160426
43198CB00022B/2966